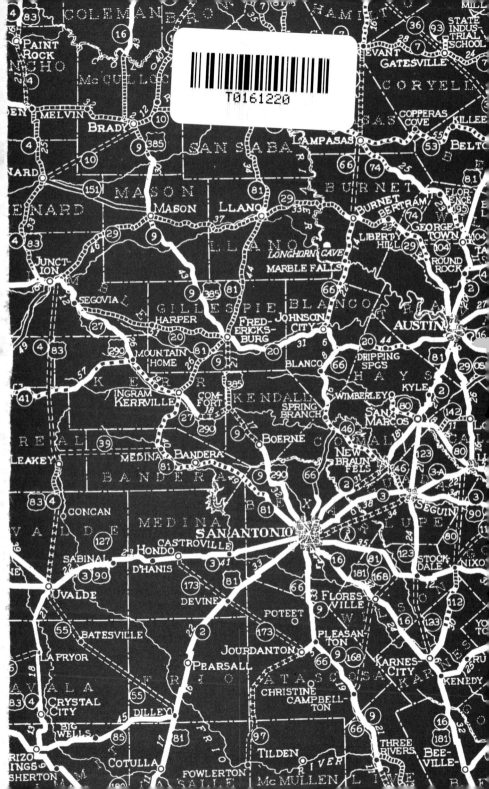

SUPERNATURAL TEXAS

Supernatural
TEXAS

50 CHILLING TALES
FROM THE
LONE STAR STATE

WILLIAM EDWARD SYERS

EDITED BY MICHAEL J. WILSON
FOREWORD BY SARAH SYERS STARK

LeafStormPress

SANTA FE, NEW MEXICO

Supernatural Texas by William Edward Syers
Copyright © 2016 by Leaf Storm Press LLC
Foreword copyright © 2016 by Sarah Syers Stark
Editor: Michael J. Wilson

Published in the United States by
Leaf Storm Press
Post Office Box 4670
Santa Fe, New Mexico 87502
leafstormpress.com

Leaf Storm logo is a trademark of Leaf Storm Press LLC
Book Design by Stewart A. Williams
Print edition ISBN 978-0-9970207-4-8
E-book ISBN 978-1-945652-00-4

Printed in Canada

10 9 8 7 6 5 4 3 2 1

Library of Congress Control Number 2016944260
Publisher's Cataloging-in-Publication Data

Names: Syers, William Edward, 1914- | Stark, Sarah Syers.
Title: Supernatural Texas : 50 chilling tales from the Lone Star State / William
    Edward Syers ; foreword by Sarah Syers Stark.
Description: Santa Fe : Leaf Storm Press, 2016. | Originally published as Ghost
    stories of Texas: Waco, TX : Texian Press, 1981.
Identifiers: LCCN 2016944260 | ISBN 978-0-9970207-4-8 (pbk.) | ISBN 978-1-
    945652-00-4 (Kindle ebook)
Subjects: LCSH: Ghosts--Texas. | Haunted places--Texas. | Legends--United States.
    | Texas--History. | BISAC: BODY, MIND & SPIRIT / Supernatural. | BODY,
    MIND & SPIRIT / Unexplained Phenomena. | HISTORY / United States /
    State & Local / Southwest (AZ, NM, OK, TX). | SOCIAL SCIENCE / Folklore
    & Mythology.
Classification: LCC BF1472.U6 S9 2016 (print) | LCC BF1472.U6 (ebook) | DDC
    133.1/09764--dc23.

FOREWORD

In my mind I see him in his red VW camper backing out of the gravel onto Thompson Drive. Kerrville, Texas. It is 1976. I am ten.

He is all packed up and ready to go—his Airedale, Casey, sits tall in the passenger seat, his deeply stained thermos mug is full of a concoction of iced tea and grape juice (stronger stuff stashed somewhere for when sunset comes)—on the road again to search down another lead for his growing collection. My grandmother has come out on the front porch to water her nasturtiums and mint, and to wave good-bye. He'll be gone at least two weeks.

William Edward Syers (Ed, to most who knew him) was a writer as long as I knew him, working on his manual Remington typewriter out in his wood-shingled writing shed near the garden, beyond the patio for long stretches most every day. Many years before that, when my mother was a teenager and he'd had his fill of *Mad Men*–style advertising in Austin, and he'd found as well that his time in the Pacific Ocean chasing Japanese submarines haunted him still, he had begun to write. Novels and histories and satires and travel guides and, eventually, these stories of ghosts.

My grandfather's efforts to gather and document and articulate these stories of ghosts and hauntings and phantoms, stories often told him by firsthand witnesses but also stories requiring additional research into the history of the locale, requiring a storyteller's ear, requiring an artist's eye, these efforts are the ones that most inhabit my memories of him. For as I've said, I was ten and eleven and twelve years old at the time.

These were the stories my grandfather began to tell around the campfire in the 1970s to me and my brother and sister and to many of our friends in the hill country surrounding Dripping Springs. He had a presence that was larger than life, and a voice that commanded attention. His face, punctuated by ice-blue eyes, could not hide the fact that he had seen a lot in his lifetime.

Originally of Jackson, Tennessee, and, as an undergraduate, the editor of the *Daily Texan* at the University of Texas ("the University," as he called it), my grandfather was never the type to hug me and compliment my drawings or my dress or my pretty smile. Instead, he was the single-most likely person to send shivers down my spine. It is probable that he alone is the reason I have never had the courage to watch horror movies, because as a child I lay awake in my bed many nights, fearing that the drumbeat sound in my inner ear was actually the Searcher of whom he had spoken so many times, a sly chuckle in his throat. In short, his stories haunted me. His very visage contained the possibility that ghosts were real, that he'd witnessed hauntings, and that he himself shivered at the thought of certain solitary roads. The possibility that his ranting might scare me, his innocent granddaughter? Well, that didn't stop him.

How appropriate then, that yesterday as I sat down to begin writing this foreword to this new edition of his *Ghost Stories of Texas*, I should look out my window toward the snow-capped Sangre de Cristos and see stopped momentarily at the street corner in front of my house, an old red VW camper van. Paused inexplicably for me to see, it looked to be packed up and ready to go, urging me as a friendly specter might, to get on with the business of writing. To pass along his original work so that a whole new generation might share his stories, might imagine his blue eyes, might shiver at the suggestion of his voice, telling these tales around the campfire.

Sarah Syers Stark
Santa Fe, New Mexico
July 2016

TABLE OF CONTENTS

THE PARTNERS

The Croton Breaks, Dickens County

Y ou may be able to find the cottonwood. I couldn't. Once it guarded a long-ago dugout and a promising spring. It was far northwest in the heaving emptiness near Spur, edging the Croton Breaks east of Lubbock—a lonely land.

I can understand those who find peace in that loneliness, a hard kind of beauty that resides where the sky is vast, distance is incalculable, and sound—other than the wind—is a stranger. Yet, you may be among those others who see land that is unforgiving of trespass. If so, you will understand the few who sense that by night it becomes a domain where the wolf still cries to the moon and restless ghosts stalk the harsh and windy dark.

Such solitude must have existed since the beginning of time, and I suppose that possibly it could have driven some men to insanity, which is what this story may relate. Near this aged tree, you see, a headless phantom eternally hunts his killer. And obviously the cottonwood must be there, because on the darkest of nights that murderer yet hangs to the gallows of its branches.

To understand what happened we must retreat over a century to when, beneath the Caprock bluffs, today's Dickens County was a land some early Texans believed they could tame.

Two of those early ones—buffalo hunters who, like most, longed to be ranchers—concern us. Call one of them Cass and the other Ike. We don't want their real names. Cass, you see, had his head severed and now roams the night without it. Ike hanged himself to the cottonwood. They found a spring full-flowing under a hummocky bluff, and there the two men—almost alone in a rolling sea of red, gritty land and mesquite—sank their dugout and set up squatters' rights to what they would call their "Cottonwood Claim."

To dress up the claim, Cass planted a cottonwood sapling beside the dugout. Here they would forget the meager rewards of the buffalo hunt; here they could envision their horizon-wide spread, their thousands of cattle. Life would be rich and good.

Nights within their dugout when icy-fingering winds bent their lamplight and the rooftree groaned under new snow, they saw only this country's promise. Their talk of it was sparse. So long together, each knew the other's thoughts before spoken. It was indeed the right comradeship for men born to be lonely.

Or so, certainly, Ike had always felt. What could intrude on two friends who saw eye-to-eye on everything and knew only the horizon for a fence line? He was so sure of this that he did not observe what must have been minute changes stealing over his partner.

Their cottonwood had grown—much larger now—when the restlessness in Cass began to surface. The 1880s were well on, and there was talk of a settlement crowding them from above, even a name for it and its county—Dickens. There were ranches coming—the big Spur closest. Land that had cost them nothing suddenly was worth money.

More money than they were grubbing out here! Cass's announcement staggered his partner. In the dugout lamplight he was suggesting selling out. He'd like a trip back East. It would be fine to see a city room for a change. It wasn't so far to Dodge, even Kansas City. No!

His partner was crazy! Ike exploded. But Cass just looked up at the sagging rooftree.

In silence, Ike turned on his bedroll and, in time, pretended to sleep. But between them, in the blackness of that dugout, a change had crept, and he knew it. Something terrible was happening to their partnership. In the morning he confronted Cass. They must hold the Cottonwood—too much had gone into it. Besides, what could be better than the life they had? City lights, his partner replied. Whiskey and women and all would be better. They must sell!

"We don't leave!" Ike said flatly.

"I intend to," Cass retorted.

There was finality in the silence that followed: the break was complete, and both of them knew it.

As the days passed, that break widened. Together as strangers now, the two men kept at their work, but they did not speak. Their dugout had become sullen, their food tasteless, their once-open range an oppressive enclosure.

In the tiny town to the east, there was talk of two crazy men over on that gravelly draw. Never a word passed between them, and no wonder—God knows how long they'd put up with each other.

Cass must have started it. Twilight was coming on, and as Ike chopped firewood, he worked with his shovel on a dead stump near their dugout. Without looking up, he finally broke the long silence. He was leaving in the morning.

With a fearful cry and too much emotion, Ike swung his chopping ax and killed Cass with a single blow. Then, aghast at what he saw and still hearing the cut-off scream, he dragged his partner beside the bluff and buried him. He had to go back for the head.

In the dugout that night, Ike stared across at the empty chair, then tensed. Outside he heard gravel crunch under a familiar tread. But only the night waited outside. It, and the shadow of Cass's cottonwood tree. Was that a cry—someone calling his name—away in the gloom? No, it was the wind. It had to be. Maybe a drink would help.

He got away from the dugout with first light, riding for the rolling horizon. On a rise he reined up to the sound of hoofbeats overtaking him. He had to make himself look around—Cass couldn't be there. And he wasn't. Still, a drink did help.

But his partner was outside the dugout that night, that creak of saddle leather, the metallic whisper of spurs. Ike lurched for the door, but Cass barred the way, just standing there with no head. It took plenty more whiskey to sleep that night.

Yet in the days and nights that followed, whiskey wouldn't drive Cass away. He rode alongside, no matter which trail Ike took. He came into the dugout each night, and there he sat, just watching Ike . . . if you could say that for something with no head. For sure, Ike knew he was losing his mind.

Over in the little town, there were rumors: Ike had gone crazy, a drunk old man, alone in the middle of nowhere. Must have run his partner off, they guessed. Who'd want to live around a man as loco as that? Occasional passing riders said he never stopped talking to himself, and the only work he seemed to do was to pile rocks up alongside a bluff by that cottonwood spring.

When Ike finally rode in to confess the murder, the sheriff listened politely. Who wouldn't feel sorry for a crazy man? Of course he understood about that headless rider. You bet it strained a man mightily when some headless fellow came into the dugout and sat down opposite you. Sure, he'd ride over to Cottonwood Claim one day soon and take a look around, if that was what Ike wanted.

But when the lawman finally rode over, it was too late. For there was Ike's body hanging from that cottonwood. He should have locked the old man up for his own safekeeping.

The sheriff was late that night in getting home, and it took a while for his wife to get the worry out of him. Oh, he knew he was hearing the wind, but it did sound like somebody kept calling Ike's name. And there were times when he looked back to see who was following: you know how a dark night can play tricks on your eyes. That's the way he reassured the rancher a few days later when the man swore he saw Ike's body still hanging from that cottonwood. Didn't the man remember helping him take Ike down to bury him by the spring?

After that Dickens County folk didn't talk much about what might be up Presslar's Draw. You have the feeling that not many get over that way, not after night closes in. As I said, it's remote country.

When I visited, I didn't wait for dark. Since I couldn't find the cottonwood, why wait for something to find me? Besides, I had a first-rate camp off to the east at White River Lake . . . and why waste a good night's sleep?

WATCHERS FROM THE WALL

near Bay City, Matagorda

I have a psychic friend who believes that at the instant of some deaths—violent ones, generally—there occurs an explosion of such intense emotion as to leave an enduring imprint on nearby surroundings, much as a flash of light would affect camera film. Pure, untested conjecture, he admits, yet it leads us to this next story in a house not far from Bay City. It was a comfortably handsome house, pink brick and dark-stained wood, a bit rambling, and certainly one that the casual passerby would never view as haunted. Yet haunted it was, in its way more so than any I had seen in Texas.

In that house lived the very real Stacey family—the husband, Bob, and wife, Eva, and two of their four children. But in addition to the Staceys, other presences abided there. There was a woman, a long-haired beauty, and a man, not quite so distinct, and, quite possibly, their child. They were seen too often and by too many to discount it. What they did to the Stacey household—none of it more harmful than a sudden startling that disrupts tranquil living—requires more space than this story is allowed.

But most incredible of all—and here, my psychic friend's theory seems to emerge—their forms and features gradually materialized on the wood paneling of the Stacey living room over several years like a slowly developing photograph.

In 1966, not long after the house was built, Bob's father visited and became absorbed with the living room's north wall paneling, near the hallway. The wood grain was changing, he insisted. The face of a young woman was taking form. No one else could see it, and so the matter was dismissed, as were the little disturbances that had begun. Untouched doors opened and closed. Dishes rattled in an empty kitchen. Household articles were moved. Lights came on and off.

"In 1974," Bob Stacey told me, "it seemed that the woman's face suddenly came into focus. All at once, we could all see her, and there was a brightness in the panel all about her face."

He saw me studying the definite aura about that face. "Would you believe that her eyes were closed at first?"

The woman's eyes were wide open, and looking directly at me.

"They follow you around the room," he added, watching me. "The man—full length, there on her right—isn't as easily seen, at least not yet. He began about the same time." He looked about his comfortable home. "So did everything else."

Eva was the first to take the visitants seriously. She returned home from a shopping trip to hear someone inside but to find no one was there. Shortly afterward, she returned to the house so briefly that she left the front door ajar. On leaving again, she found it locked from the inside. Still, she could find no one home. Some time after that, Eva was gathering clothes to be washed and, turning toward the hall, she saw a tall, slender young woman pass her doorway. Rushing to it, she found nothing but empty hallway. But she knew what she had seen. It was the woman whose face was now clear on the living room paneling.

Bob's acceptance came soon after that. One evening after work, he relaxed by the television with his son, the only other family member in the house. Then in the hallway, he heard a woman begin to hum. Could Eva have returned? He called, and then looked, but no one was there. Perplexed, he returned to the couch, and then was thunderstruck with the appearance of two legs, mid-thigh down, walking into the room, standing before him for a moment before vanishing.

That night, his daughter awakened to see two shadows against her bedroom wall. They touched, as though in embrace, then vanished. She lay still in her bed, knowing what had waked her. The shadows had been talking. A woman and a man.

Later, a man's disembodied head drifted down the hallway.

His son soon confirmed both presences as well, each appearing while he talked on the phone. As the son sat on the bed, a middle-aged man walked directly between his startled gaze and the wall and disappeared, apparently through the wall. The second visitation came while the son was in the kitchen. Some cold sense made him turn around sharply, and there she was: the long-haired woman standing in front of him for an instant before disappearing.

"This has been happening for about nine years," Bob Stacey told me. "As nearly as we can make it out, they moved into this home while we were away. I was in Alice on a job for more than six months, and the house was empty. When we got back, they were definitely here." He thought back. "Things would be quiet for two or three months, and we'd think they'd gone away, but they hadn't."

At first when things seemed to get out of hand, the family would leave the house for the sanctuary of a motel. But little by little they realized that the apparitions meant no harm, and so they simply stuck it out. They did this through manifestations that, although invisible, were as extraordinary as the visitants' appearances.

Bob, seated on the bed, believed he felt his wife sit down opposite his turned back. But when he turned around to speak to her, he found no one on the bed, and the room empty. In their game room, at the pool table, an unseen guest joined in the game, sometimes tossing balls out of the pocket and back onto the table. Other times a missed shot, motionless on the table, suddenly steered itself into a pocket. More than once, the game room lights turned on and the table played itself after the family went to bed.

A visiting cousin, resting from shooting baskets outside, was confronted with a basketball as it seemingly dribbled itself from its shelf, around two corners, straight down the hall, finally to the corner once more to rest at the feet of the unnerved young man.

A visiting aunt walked from the kitchen with a glass of water only to have the glass whisked from her hand midway down the dark hall. "To this day," Bob Stacey said, "We've never found the glass, nor any place where water was spilled . . . and the house was locked. They seem to like playing with water," he added. "They cut off the hot while you're showering, things like that. One night in that hallway—I was alone and it was dark—a glass of water flew right into my face." He shook his head. "From nowhere."

Not all the spectral pranks are playful, however. Once, when the Stacey son was practicing his drums—"I suppose it was pretty loud," his father admitted—the facing of the living room air conditioner flew off as though hurled across the room, while a large heavy planter was tossed on its side.

Again, there was no visible being in the room. No one nearby.

Before I left, Bob listed a score of other incidents, many of them leading to his conviction that a child was with the man and woman even though it had yet to appear on the wood paneling.

Stacey shook his head. "The man and the woman only. They seem to get clearer, little by little. But maybe it's my imagination."

What did the Staceys do with their home? They continued to dwell in it; they'd put too much into its building to leave. And there had been no harm done to them.

Who were these ghosts? Where did they come from?

About 1830, according to an old story, a family came picnicking up from the tiny, just-founded little coastal town of Matagorda. They disappeared close by this spot, goes the tale, never again to be seen or heard from.

"There were no newspapers then, and the really old-timers are long gone," Bob Stacey thought aloud. "Who knows?"

Of course I agreed with him. But on leaving, I took one last look at the lovely, long-haired lady on the wood paneling. Sure enough, her eyes had followed me to the door.

THE NIGHT RIDERS OF
STAMPEDE MESA

Kalgary, Post, Spur

The end of the 1800s was a long time ago, and the man's name is lost, even to old-timers who once knew of the killer stampede. Along the dusty trails that crawl up from the breaks country to the Caprock and High Plains beyond, names have a way of fading out. Or perhaps cattlemen do not like to admit to ghosts. Even the guilty mesa is becoming difficult to locate.

Under the Panhandle, down from Crosbyton in the direction of Spur, the lush green plains break off sharply. Below, the red and gray land heaves in repetitious rims and hills, low against the sky. On a backroad to Post, near little Kalgary, lies the jumbled canyon of the White River. This is near the place. Up-canyon toward the White River Reservoir, you can make out the hunched hills and mesas of the old L-Seven Ranch. That is the ghost ground, many years ago given its name by able cowboy folklorist John Craddock.

Old-timers might, if they choose, direct you there on horseback. You'd likely arrive just before dark, though. It is then that the mesa's ghost riders descend upon any who intrude. However discounted these days, the story insists that they intend to take you over a hundred-foot cliff.

The cattle were close-packed as they stormed out that night more than a hundred years ago, their wet backs sleek, their eyes orange and wild, fireballs riding their horns, the very ground shaking beneath them. And they came upon the cliff with no ground for the riders to turn them. The chief drover watched from below, horrified, as two riders were swept over the cliff amidst the herd's cascade, along with most of his herd. And then in cold terror he saw the ones who had driven them—the dead nester and his ghost cows. Luminous, they floated right to the edge, hung momentarily against the black sky, and then vanished.

The next morning, sick with his mangled beef, sicker with the two riders he buried in the lean breaks below the cliff, the drover looked up just once. Above him, the mesa hunched enigmatically, offering no answers.

The mesa, according to Craddock, took its name in a fashion that was macabre even in the hard days of early trail drives. The possibility of stampede was known to every trail driver—few indeed were the herds that did not, at least once, explode in blind, thundering terror. A hat in the wind, a sneeze, a sudden laugh, a gunshot. Even something as trivial as a rolling, gust-blown tumbleweed could loose the millrace. Why even mention lightning or jayhawkers?

But ghosts?

It started with the drover named Jones who trailed through to the plains in the 1880s. He had over a thousand head, slaty from the long dry traverse and a little spooky with it too. Jones planned to make for what promised to be good bedding ground for his herd that night on the mesa. For the mesa led down to water across a small neck of land, and though its broad grassland ended in sheer cliff, Jones felt it would serve as a strong boundary, better than a fence.

He did not know that he was about to leave this trail a fearful legacy.

Near his destination, Jones was met by a nester driving a few steers out of the brush. They looked poor to Jones. As he would tell it later, he only shrugged when the stranger flanked them right into his own big herd.

That the man had figured to pick up extra head was obvious, as Jones told it. The nester said he had the lead on the trail toward that bedding ground, but he'd just take his cows and be on his way instead. Already, Jones would claim, the stranger was cutting out some of the big trail herd.

Jones rested his rifle across his saddle horn, saying the nester's cows would bed right along with the big herd, and he could cut them in the morning. There wasn't time now before dark. Though the stranger protested, Jones persisted. And so they watered the herd together and just before dark pushed up into the high grass to camp for the night. The cattle were contented and drowsy, and all seemed quiet.

But deep into the small hours, a blind stampede exploded. They ran not in the direction of the water below, but straight for the cliffs. One of Jones's riders who didn't ride over the cliff tried to reconstruct what had happened. He thought he had seen the nester riding the onrush, waving and shooting. Furious, Jones rode the nester down. They tied the man to his horse and blindfolded both, then pitched mount and rider off into the abyss.

After that, drovers shunned that tableland. Most cowmen knew that once trouble picks a spot, it settles there. Still, the grass and water were too much for some to resist, and across night campfires, the story began to grow.

Bed a herd up there and you'd lose everything. That nester and his ghost cows had been seen more than once. He came out of the night, calling for his cattle. He came down on you, fighting his ropes and choking on his gag. He came straight for the cliffs, somehow floating his herd through the night, and he swept everything over along with him. Old trail hands no longer scoffed at ghost yarns when, over the years, one then another rider died in the night on the rocks below Stampede Mesa.

Finally no one at all camped that high ground. Of course, the trail drives were about done by the 1900s, and maybe the nester came back just to wreak his vengeance on cattlemen, and on them alone. But then, who is able to predict such a ghost?

If you're game to have a look, there's camping at nearby White River Reservoir, where you'd be in the mesa's general vicinity. My last night there, the wind was right and occasional lightning flared away to the southwest. There was no question about the low thunder coming from around Stampede Mesa. Who'd be up there, contending with that nester? Had all those ghost riders come back, still protecting their herds?

EDITOR'S NOTE: Though not commonly used today, the word *drover* refers to a person who drives groups of animals (often sheep or cattle) from one place to another. *Nesters* is what the cattlemen called settlers or homesteaders, who often charged fees for cattle passing through their land or for releasing trespassing cattle.

THE BRUJA'S WEB

Seguin

Around the old land of Las Norias, deep in South Texas, and long ago around the campfires of the vaqueros on land that is now within the confines of the King Ranch, the *bruja* is considered a very real creature, and much to be feared. There are those who have seen her high in the night sky, a dark shadow against the moon.

Many might confuse the *bruja* with a mere witch, but to those minds more finely tuned to the infinite, she is understood as something unique, possessing an array of cunning devices. There is something of Caribbean voodoo in her practice, an ability to reach vengeance across space and time, a dark skill that the ancients—from the Hawaiian Islands to the Balkans and to Africa—may understand, but rarely discuss. She is known to undergo a self-transformation when it serves her purpose, usually to a *lechuza*, or screech owl. In this way she may undertake long journeys, flying high over the housetops.

I mention all of this because in the Rio Grande Valley from Brownsville to McAllen, this creature has appeared on more than one police blotter.

When John Paul Amador was a child his family experienced the *bruja* at close range. Living in Houston at the time, his father was employed by the city and worked hard to support his family. Still, when their quiet neighbor asked to borrow money, the Amadors agreed. She seemed a nice-enough woman, and no doubt would repay the loan. But in fact, when John's mother approached the woman several times, explaining that repayment was needed, the neighbor refused.

"She told my mother," John recalled, "that my mother had made a bad mistake, insisting on it—that something was going to happen to her. Of course, none of us paid any attention to that . . . not at the time."

Almost immediately, however, John's mother became ill, losing weight, growing weaker by the day. The doctor said there was nothing really wrong with her, but it might be that living in a big city upset her. So the family, all but the father who had to stay in Houston for work, moved to Seguin where they owned a little second house. But even in Seguin, John's mother did not improve.

It was not long before John and his sisters and mother knew they'd been beset by something evil. "I remember that right at twilight one day, we were all in the yard, playing, and this big *lechuza*—you know, a screech owl—suddenly flew down and crouched in the highest branches of our big hackberry tree. It just sat there watching us, and then it began to make these awful noises."

After that, strangeness descended upon them.

Precisely at sunset each day, the great bird was there, high up on the same limb. When darkness came, the mother and children—all of them awake and waiting—began to hear the noises: voices outside when no one was there. A rattling on the walls—not just one wall, but on all four sides of the house simultaneously.

"There would come this sharp scraping on the screen of my window," John said. "I could look straight out of it; nobody was there. And it was happening at every window."

John and his sisters—Isabel, Beatriz, Dolores, and little Maria—did not become frightened until two things became clear to them. One was the undeviating schedule of the owl's appearance: each twilight, Monday through Friday, it was there, watching. Yet, when their father came from Houston on weekends, it was gone. "I'm not sure he believed us," John said. "Maybe that was part of the woman's plan."

He went on to explain what happened when night fell.

"It was like a wall of darkness closed us off." He spread his hands. "You know how people in a small neighborhood like this like to visit one another. Just drop by—they always had, before. But after dark, not one soul ever came to our house. It was like we were cut off from the world."

A web of darkness.

"You could look out the window—knowing there was a neighbor's house right there—and yet you couldn't really see that house. You couldn't see the one next door, only twenty feet away. You couldn't see where, in the daylight, we played across the street."

On Saturdays, when their father was home, the neighbors started visiting again, and the kids could see out the windows. Everything was normal. When he would return to Houston, the craziness would begin again. At sunset on Monday, the owl arrived at the tree, and the Amador kids would move indoors. John claimed that once inside, they couldn't even hear the kids playing across the street.

It wasn't clear whether the owl was visible to anyone outside the family. And wouldn't that be the perfect way to drive someone mad?

Finally John's mother asked advice from friends. They told her to put limes and crosses over the door, the windows, and the beds. It seemed to help, although there was one last visitation.

The five children had been playing just at sunset and then looked up to see the owl in the big tree. Without warning, it flew straight down and attacked them. Their mother had to beat it off and get the children into the house.

After that, it never came back, and they learned later that it was around that time that the old neighbor lady in Houston had died. I asked John if he believed the woman had been a *bruja*. "I'm a business man," John said, "I'm just telling you what happened."

Still, John admits, the Amadors kept those crosses and limes posted for a long time even after the old woman had died.

THE BOY

Geronimo, Guadalupe County

In setting down these stories, I have given considerable thought to what we call psychic powers. To my mundane mind, their possessors are like intricate receivers, able to tune so finely that they pick up signals that are indistinguishable to the rest of us.

To this latter group, I am reasonably sure I belong. On the other hand, I feel certain that Mrs. Lucille White of Johnson City was psychic to a marked degree. She was a trim, attractive lady with a direct way of speaking and a gaze that, at first, I would have described with the same term.

Yet I think that Lucille White's inner eyes saw more than most; she could tune to that infinitely remote transmitter. She came by this, apparently, from a family sensitive to things extraterrestrial—supernatural, if you prefer. There was no mumbo jumbo about her. In her home near the town's school, she went about raising her family and living her life in a manner as normal as any.

However, during a long morning visit, she told me a number of stories—as matter-of-factly as one would describe a trip to the store—that leave little doubt but that the unusual was somewhat routine in her experience. She was conscious of her gift . . . if you choose to call it that.

She became aware of this psychism through her mother and a particular incident that occurred in the early 1900s.

Little Geronimo was a wayside village beside a creek in the broad and rich meadowland just north of Seguin. Lucille's mother, Ada, was a girl in her teens when her family, the Ludwig Neumann family, farming people, moved into a big house on the south edge of that town. Those who had rented the place before the Neumanns were closemouthed about their leaving. But a rumor persisted that "someone else" lived there, too. It had so frightened one of the boys that he had fired a shot through his locked door, wounding his brother.

But Ludwig Neumann was a practical man of the earth, and farming was his family's daylight-to-dark occupation. Before long, his daughters, including young Ada, forgot stories of the big house's other dweller.

The girl's first encounter came on a misty September evening. The chores were done, and a friend was coming over to visit. To await her friend on the porch, Ada left the family in the kitchen and crossed the darkened living room. In the middle of that room, a sudden chill enveloped her. Then something cold touched her cheek. It was the thing in the house! She ran, but the porch was black dark, so she could not stay there.

To reach her family meant recrossing that room, and Ada did. This time there was no mistaking the other presence. A hand, ice-cold, brushed her face, and she bit back a scream. Then she was with her family again, the lights were brightly reassuring, and there were all her sisters who surely would tease her if she mentioned her experience. So she said nothing about the dark room.

A few nights later, Ada was no longer alone in awareness of the presence. One sister who had gone out to empty the dishwater returned hurriedly, her eyes wide. She, too, said nothing, for the other two Neumann sisters were outside bringing in the laundry from the line.

The lamp, atop a cabinet on the porch, threw a little circle of light as the girls began to work. Then they stopped abruptly: beyond the reach of that lamplight, something was walking near the buggy house beside the windmill. They worked faster.

Then they saw it. From the line of brush by the windmill, it emerged—hazy white and luminescent. Slowly at first, it came toward them. They ran for the house.

From the porch, a terrified backward glance showed the thing, utterly formless, close enough to reach for them. They burst in to the house, the still-burning lamp forgotten outside.

These two didn't try to hide what had happened to them. They told their story to the family—the thing had chased them! It was then that the first sister broke her silence—it had chased her, too.

But what was it? It was hazy. How could they know when they ran so fast? It seemed small, almost like a boy. Most of all, it moved faster than anyone could run and it got close . . . so close!

They decided their father should go back for the lamp. He didn't take his gun because he was sure the girls were seeing things in the dark.

But when he returned with the lamp, there was a look in his eyes that Ada had never seen before. He explained that the double doors, the ones on the side that had been jammed shut for the entire time they'd lived there, now stood wide open.

They guessed that it, whatever it was, had come inside. Throughout the house, they turned up all the lamps and left them lighted. Ludwig Neumann cleaned his gun. But when morning came, nothing seemed to have happened. Ada knew what had happened; the thing had returned outside.

A week later, the Neumanns' married daughter, Bertha, came for a visit. Eldest of all the girls, she shamed her sisters for overactive imaginations. Ghosts? Nonsense.

But that night, as Bertha cooled her feet in a pan of cold water on the front porch, her meditation time became a time for terror. First, she saw the buggy house door open slowly. Then it burst wide, its interior a black pit. Out of that pit a hazy figure emerged and, before Bertha's horrified eyes, it took form.

She sat transfixed, prayer forming on her lips, for she could distinguish what she saw. This was a small creature, a boy glowing translucent with—it would later confound her to have noticed it—very large shoes, shoes far too big for him.

How could she have noticed the shoes? The boy—he seemed momentarily busy at the woodpile—had no head. No head at all!

Then he turned on her and came running for the porch.

She burst screaming into the house: "It has no head! It has no head!"

Again, the Neumann lamps came on, and with all his strength, Ludwig Neumann jammed those double doors closed. There was nothing inside. Nothing outside either, he confirmed, returning this time with his gun and his face pale.

Still, Bertha was not the last to encounter Geronimo's headless boy.

The Neumann house, large as it was, was the place for choir practice. Families from many nearby fields came regularly to sing Gesangbuch's old songs. Perhaps thirty singers had gathered in the big room just off the downstairs hall this particular night. Ludwig Neumann and his wife sat closest to the hallway door, so they could both join the singing and manage the household.

They saw him first. At the double doors that Ludwig Neumann had this time wedged closed, there was sudden noise: the sound of someone bounding up the steps and across the dark porch. Silently, effortlessly, those doors opened wide. And in the doorway stood the boy. Straight down the hallway he came—not walking, simply moving soundlessly. Straight past the thunderstruck parents and the horrified gaze of those within the choir room who fell silent.

The boy carried something—a pillow? Or something wrapped in a pillowcase? In a flash he was beyond the choir room door and up the steps to the second floor. To the day she died, Ada was never certain whether his head was on his shoulders or in the pillowcase he carried.

Ludwig Neumann, reeling to his feet, rushed for the stairway, the men of the choir close behind. Every upstairs room was vacant. And nothing had come down that staircase.

Not too long afterward, the Neumanns moved; Ludwig was getting too old to farm, he told his family. And maybe that was the reason. They never went back and, near Geronimo's gravel pit, the old house is long gone.

Why was the boy there?

"An unfinished life," Lucille White answered quickly. "A violent end to it."

What had severed the head? No one knew; they hadn't thought much beyond the frightfulness of what they all saw.

Since then, Lucille White had learned that the Geronimo area, like all of Guadalupe County, was an area of great violence between the Comanche and Anglo settlers during those ten years of the Texas Republic (1836-1846). There were many civilian deaths, including those of children, on both sides of that conflict. As well, close by on the old Timmerman place, there once had been a Lipan Apache campground. The big shoes on the boy could have been crudely fashioned moccasins, outgrown and passed on.

Somewhere near that little village, a headless boy may still appear. To some, that is, who have eyes to see him.

THE NIGHT CALL

San Antonio

Quite purposely, it seemed, the stranger stood in the late-night shadows outside, his hat pulled low, his face obscured. In a hollow voice, he said that the emergency was south, below the new homes down Flores and Presa Streets. He needed the doctor's help.

That the doctor was about to embark on a house call he would never forget, to venture into a yet-unexplained mystery, did not occur to the young San Antonio physician. It was the new century of the 1900s, and he had a promising practice in this growing little city of fifty thousand, and a pretty young wife—altogether a good life.

It was a fine night, the night it happened. The moon was soft and the green scent of spring was in the air. Even though it was late, he invited his wife to come along for the ride.

He turned to reassure the stranger who had come knocking at their door, but the man had retreated into the dark at the hitching post and was already saddled. Silent, he waited there, then led the way down South Presa, where only a few lamplight windows still watched the night.

"What's wrong with him?" The doctor's wife seemed uneasy. "He's so withdrawn."

"His friend's hurt. He's worried. You could tell it in his voice. With night calls, they're always worried."

The physician flicked his reins to keep up as his wife wondered about the stranger's old-fashioned clothing. The horseman was indistinct in the night ahead of them, traveling farther than the doctor had expected. The fine two-story houses had thinned to scattered frame bungalows. Then the cobbled paving stopped, and off to the east, the dark line of river timber crept closer. Now the shadowy rider took a narrow side road leading into those trees.

It was dark beneath them—clouds had scudded across the moon. They scarcely saw the man dismount, for suddenly the house loomed. Deep in the trees it stood—four square columns, a broad front gallery, and gabled windows—all of it vaguely brooding.

As though part of their surrounding shadows, the man stood motionless within a near grove of oaks. Without speaking, he pointed toward one dimly-lighted window. The physician, with deliberate effort, put down an uneasiness that was growing. He spoke quietly to his wife, saying she should stay in the buggy.

He mounted the steps to the porch and found the front door ajar. The lighted room was just off the entrance hall, so dark he could distinguish nothing within it. Bag in hand, he entered the dim room, unprepared for what awaited him. Blood, in gouts and spatters, seemed everywhere. A chair, its leg broken off, sagged in the corner. To the doorway where he stood, a bloody trail led from a bed across the room. A table beside it had been overturned.

On the bed, a young woman lay still, watching him. Under her right kneecap was a smear of blood.

Even with the woman before him and his thoughts racing, the mind of a physician prevailed—someone had just died here. The feel of it seeped in from the dark all about, an intimate violence.

But he reminded himself: the woman was wounded; he must treat her. She was naked. Someone should be with him—his wife? He turned toward the window, but a voice challenged from the darkness beyond: "Leave her out here!"

The doctor opened his bag and bent over the woman on the bed.

The wound was slight, so he treated and bandaged it, working rapidly. Silent, the woman's eyes remained on him. He felt them, though he could not hear her breathe.

"It's not too bad," he said, seeing a bullet had grazed her. Feeling the hair crawl along his neck, he hurried to finish. From the corner of his eye, he had glimpsed a face at the window—momentarily there, and then gone.

He told the woman to come to his office the next morning. He would redress the wound. Without speaking, she nodded. It was only when he turned at the door that he realized how extraordinarily pretty she was. Then the deadliness of the room and the sense of imminent violence beset him again, and he plunged into the dark hall and safely through it.

He forced himself not to run for his buggy. Then he was in it, almost unaware that from somewhere in the shadows, money had been thrust into his hand. He reined around, feeling his wife trembling, and he looked back only once as he whipped the horse.

Night swallowed the house. The light at that solitary window was extinguished.

His wife was desperately afraid. A man had watched the doctor work from the window. Not the one who had come to their home: that one had stayed in the trees. But another man at the window, with a gun.

He told her what he had seen. Someone had been murdered and dragged out.

Two days passed while he waited for the young woman to come for an examination. She would never come. Then, he went to the police.

There was nothing at that address, a deputy told him—just an old house that hadn't been occupied in years. It was not old, the doctor insisted; he had been there. He would show them.

In the end, two officers went with him. There was no mistaking the lonely road or the house, almost as shadowy by day as he remembered it.

But that was all that he had remembered correctly. It was a sagging wreck of abandonment.

And that room. The bed was there, and the chair and bedside table. A coverlet lay on the bed, unstained. Everywhere, dust spread an undisturbed mantle. The doctor rubbed his eyes—this had been the slaughterhouse room.

There were stains on the flooring that had been scrubbed many times . . . but long ago. The gallery sagged as they came out to speak to the deputy who had waited outside. He hurried over, shaking his head in disbelief.

The deputy explained that as he'd been waiting, all at once in the closest grove of trees, a man had been watching him. There was blood all over his face, and his shirt was soaked with it. As the deputy had started for him, the man had disappeared.

"Not twenty feet from me, plain as day," the deputy said. "Then he vanished!"

They prowled all through the trees toward the river but found nothing. No one.

Returning to town, the doctor put his question hesitantly—did they believe what he had told them? To himself he admitted that he was no longer sure of what he had seen, and he chose not to return to the house.

The officers remained noncommittal, and came the next day to look again more closely. The deputy knew what he had seen—a dead man still on his feet.

Shortly thereafter, the officers closed their investigation. There was talk—secondhand, as is the way with such talk—that the officers had seen the bloody figure waiting in the grove once more, and among themselves, had agreed to leave the story alone and close the case.

As so the house remained empty, and the case closed. A short time later, a flood took the ruin away. Where its foundations had stood, some said that a grave-sized hole remained. Others thought the grave was nearer the trees by the house . . . but floodwaters do strange things to bottomland.

Some say, even today, that the doctor's descendants still possess three silver dollars—payment for a late-night house call. Who can be sure?

Doctors have a rule—they must never talk about the patients they have treated.

LAS CHIMENEAS

Eagle Pass, Piedras Negras

Back in the 1920s Jovita Gonzales, an able folklorist from Roma, downriver, unearthed the old story. It went like this.

In the vast sea of brush some twenty miles northeast of then tiny Eagle Pass, the hunter was lost. The drear November twilight with its cold misting rain enveloped him that night. Through the mesquite and guajillo and catclaw, he must have circled many times. Either that, or there was no house, no living being, within miles.

It was then that he came upon the shepherd, old and bent, driving his small flock. That man's jacal would welcome the hunter for a night; indeed, for miles across this lonely land, there was no other place to stay. The old man led the way.

As night closed in on the twisting trail, an abrupt turn revealed a big house, almost obscured in heavy growth. Yet there it loomed, vaguely white, with many chimneys and with walls that, even in the gloom, revealed ruin. Still, it offered shelter, and wood was all about. The hunter thought he could warm himself by one of the fireplaces those chimneys promised.

He would stay there, the hunter told the old shepherd.

"*Señor,*" the old man whispered, "for your life, do not go in there."

Later, in the shepherd's small dwelling that night, the hunter learned of the deadly phantoms of Las Chimeneas, the aged fortress-rancho they had avoided.

Toward Crystal City some seventeen miles, then northward five more from its big, locked gate, the ruin of Las Chimeneas guarded immense, empty ranchland. The gaunt and crudely plastered rock house supported a corrugated iron roof over two rooms and a porch.

For many years hunters used the old house as make-do shelter, for there were whitetail in the brush, a man-made tank for nearby water, and electric lines to the building. Today, a renovated though still rustic structure, Las Chimeneas (now called Dos Chimeneas) remains a destination for hunters as part of the once 200,000-acre Chittim Ranch.

The men who oversee the broad Chittim holdings know the story of Las Chimeneas.

The rancho was built at the time when Spain controlled land on both sides of the Rio Grande. This hacienda belonged to a wealthy Spanish family, Vegas by name, and it was a virtual fort, with gun-ported walls about many rooms—with many chimneys, thus its name. Here, in the early 1800s, when Mexican fought Spaniard and the Lipan Apache fought both, it promised sanctuary to the Vegas family, where death awaited them across the river or too far out in the brush.

It was known that fearful violence had overtaken the Vegas family, for they disappeared, leaving only bloodstained rooms that told of desperate fighting. Known too was the fact that the Vegas wealth, spirited from Mexico, was buried close by.

Unlike those who visited Las Chimeneas by day, the old shepherd had witnessed its occupants who returned by night. Had he not driven his flock past this place countless times when dark sent him along his homeward trail? Had he not always heard violent voices within, sounds of mortal struggle, screams of death? There were those, the shepherd knew, who believed that the Apache had done this, but he believed a different story—he had heard those voices tell of treasure that someone would try to take from them. Was it not very natural that the Vegas phantoms would fall violently upon any who came upon them by night? The hunter was fortunate that the shepherd possessed lodging he would share.

Still, the shepherd's tale was discounted by many on this side of the Rio Grande as mere superstition. Among the doubters, four Texas cowboys determined to test all the foolishness about the old ruin, planned to spend the night there. With lanterns and ready revolvers, they settled in over a deck of cards.

Precisely at midnight, a sudden gust of wind blew out their lanterns. Through the dark, they heard the jingle of Chihuahua-roweled spurs. They pulled their guns then—scorning fear—relighted the lanterns. Again, their lamps snuffed out. When the front door opened, they burst out the back, and for the rest of the night they camped at a distance. From that time on, none of them would talk about Las Chimeneas, nor would they ride near it at night.

But the shepherd's story did not end there; he nearly became a wealthy man.

One evening at dusk, he pushed his flock toward the house he dreaded. The house he must pass, each homeward-bound night. This time, the inner voices were so violent, so clear, he thought for a moment that someone must have dared to enter.

That night he heard talk of fighting, of treasure, of murder for those riches that were buried beneath a nearby tree. Fearful, he hurried ahead, and drove his flock safely around a bend in the trail. But he knew that tree the voices had described, and the next morning, frightened or not, he returned with a shovel.

Only a hole awaited him. In the gray soil at its bottom he detected the imprint of a heavy chest.

Someone had been there before him!

And now? Are there no longer any Vegas ghosts? Is there nothing left for the ghosts to guard? Who disappeared all those years ago with all the gold?

No one seems to know.

EDITOR'S NOTE: Both the words *drear* and *jacal* are correct though you may be unfamiliar with them. The first, as you might guess, is a synonym of dreary. The second is a simple thatched-roof hut; most often found in the southwestern United States or in Mexico, made of sticks or poles and covered with mud or clay.

SUE

Big Spring

Since so many of us are skeptical of ghost tales—nothing but fanciful legend passed along by overactive imaginations—perhaps it's time to focus on a story closer to present—the 1970s in Big Spring. An eighteen-year-old named Robert Stephens, and his confrontation with terror from beyond.

Robert's room, paneled and carpeted, was in the precise order in which his mother always left it: bed remade, everything dusted, his stereo waiting for him to slip on the earphones. The room was empty and still. The whole neighborhood, on the east side of the city, was one of quiet homes and ordered lawns.

That night, Robert planned to read or relax, maybe listen to a little country music. First—though he was uneasy with the decision—there was something that must be done. For several weeks, the slim, tousle-haired young man had put down a mounting concern, keeping things to himself. Finally he had talked with his mother—could there be something in his room, his car, wherever he went? Was a ghost possible?

Like his father, his mother was a lifelong West Texan and devout. She reassured her son. He should speak directly to that empty room. When nothing happened, he could forget about ghosts.

For a moment Robert surveyed his silent room. Then, making his voice casual, he spoke. "Hello, whoever you are. What's your name?"

Moments later, hearing her son cry out, Robert's mother rushed in. His heavy dictionary lay on the floor at his feet. Something had picked it from his table, floated it across the room to where it lay, turned its pages methodically, and folded one page to point its fold to a single word.

Sue.

Sue, who was to dwell in the Stephens's home for several months because she was apparently "in love with Robert," had first made her presence known on a February night when Robert drove home from a basketball game. His ashtray had popped open, and the suckers he kept there were tossed out as his glove compartment flew open. He dismissed it all to a bump in the road that he had not felt.

Shortly afterward, his bedroom fan—he liked its quiet whir—had cut off, and the bedroom door had closed of its own accord. The following night this happened again. Suspecting a short, he left the fan off the third night. This time it clicked on, and again the door closed. He made himself put down a growing uneasiness.

Some days later, he sat on this bed, reading. Now there was no mistaking the chilling sense of another presence—close, as though someone had sat beside him. His eyes turned from the book to the bed. Something was lying there, full length—there was a single, clear body indentation.

It was then that he had confessed his fear to his family.

Now his mother was beside him, staring at the open dictionary. Maybe she might believe that he had placed it there himself. He asked her: was he going crazy?

He said aloud, "I wish that 'she' would prove herself to you."

With that, the birdhouse on his dresser rose from its place and floated across the room.

His mother gasped, "Oh, my God!"

In time Sue increased her determination. While the Stephens' car was in motion she would open the rear door to sit beside Robert and, still invisible, would fasten his seat belt. She would sit beside him on the bed, follow him to the movies, and take the nearest seat. She convinced his skeptical older sister by nearly pushing her off the bed. Once, after a week's vacation, the Stephens family returned to find their kitchen in disarray. At nights while they slept, they could hear the television being turned on. While they entertained in the back family room, something upended the TV set and much of the living room furniture. Another time, while the family was out, both living and dining room were reduced to shambles—all furniture turned over. When police were called to investigate, they found no fingerprints.

Then, in antique script, she began to leave messages on Robert's mirror.

I love you.

Sue was to repeat that message a dozen times and, when Robert's cousin brought a tape recorder, she spoke the words in a thin, faraway voice.

I love you.

"She was determined to prove her presence," Robert explained to me many years later. "I've prayed all my life—all my family's that way—but I never prayed as hard as then. Make her leave!"

Sue's final message, again on the mirror, drove the Stephens family nearer to crisis. "Robert, I must always be seated on your right."

What does a young man do when his world spins beyond his comprehension?

"I don't understand," the troubled youth said aloud. In his room, he turned to see Sue standing there, facing him, fully visible.

"She wore a long, shining dress that was tight in the middle," Robert recalled. "It had big sleeves, puffy. She wore a bonnet. She was about five feet five." In a plain way, he supposed, she was somewhat pretty.

For perhaps a minute or so—an eternity—she confronted Robert, telling him some of her story. She had died in 1770 at age twenty-one. She gave her full name and where she had died. Robert was too horror-struck to recall any of the details. She was not of the Devil; she only wanted acceptance. He should not fear her; she loved him.

After that she would not—or could not—materialize again.

"She wanted me to talk, I think." Robert thought back. "I couldn't open my mouth. Then, on my knees, I prayed for thirty or forty minutes for God to take her away. When I finished, I felt a sense of peace; she seemed to have left."

Disarmingly, that peace continued for several weeks. The Stephens family relaxed, hoping they were free of Sue.

They were not.

One night as Robert relaxed on his bed, earphones muting the music, his bed began to shake as though handled by someone in anger, like a toy in some giant hand. Things in his room began to fly through the air. From the opposite wall, the heavy chest of drawers careened across the room and, wedging there, blocked the door. Then the door latched, and there was no getting out or in. At the top of his voice Robert yelled against the fear.

"I guess I went to pieces," Robert confessed later. "She was locking me in."

After that the family sought help from their minister and eventually a psychiatrist. Robert agreed to face commitment at Big Spring State Hospital. On a Monday morning, a preliminary examination set admission for that afternoon, pending a final psychiatric examination. But the psychiatrist, after talking a long time with Robert, and then calling for a second opinion, declared Robert sane. He said the Stephens' problem was simple: a ghost named Sue had inhabited their home. He would be willing to help send her away.

The doctor, also a student of parapsychology, began coming to the Stephens' home on nights when not on duty. A big, forthright man, he met Sue, alone in Robert's room. His exorcism—or blessing, as some might call it—followed a direct plan. All the family would address Sue through him: he would be a psychic relay between this plane and beyond.

"We told her she couldn't stay," Robert said. "Not in our family. I told her I couldn't handle any more of this."

Through the psychiatrist, Sue replied. She understood. She had meant no harm, but she would leave. She hoped they would never forget her.

"Will you?" I asked Robert. "Will you forget her?"

"No." The word was instant.

Last time I checked, Sue had been gone for more than two years.

What about your home? Is your son of an age and sensitivity sufficient to attract such a determined young woman? While you consider that, suppose we get on with these legends that—of course—we all dismiss to fancy.

THE SENTINEL

Tehuacana, east of Waco

In fading autumn twilight, the hilltop darkened against a still red-streaked sky, the figure atop it no more than a silhouette. For half an hour, the boy had watched that figure, motionless, staring westward from the edge of a brief bluff.

The watcher was young John Boyd, son of one of his village's founders. He knew what he saw was a Native man, and that was strange, because in these late 1850s, there hadn't been one around Tehuacana in some years. From Waco, off to the west, they'd been moved out to a reservation. Slowly the boy climbed closer, and then he spoke a greeting.

An erect statue in buckskin, the man neither turned nor moved. The boy spoke again, making his voice friendly. After all, what danger could there be? Within earshot must be two dozen settlers' rifles if he called out. Besides, this strange, unmoving man could not have come for trouble; there was no nearby pony for his escape.

The village could spare food. Was he hungry? Young John had moved close now, close enough to detect the craftsmanship in the buckskins, the carefully braided black hair, and the weaponless belt. And, most of all, that strange glow about the figure. It was as though the fading light radiated through him.

And then the head turned, slowly, as though with an intense labor of will. The eyes, dark as black pits, fixed the boy. No expression crossed his face, simply the awareness of another presence. The boy felt cold all through, a cold literally projected by that gaze, and then something within John Boyd said to run. Run fast.

But before he could move, the man was gone.

The figure had vanished.

In the tiny village of Tehuacana, on its hilly ridges forty miles east of Waco, some smiled at the boy's story. A few others remembered looking up from their plows toward that hilltop—sunset or sunrise was the time they remembered—and seeing something they had later decided not to mention.

And so it was that the son of Major John Boyd, a Tehuacana founder, was the first to openly encounter the last chieftain of the Tawakoni, a man who had died in a massacre some thirty years earlier. The boy was the first, but would not be the last to see the hilltop sentinel. For years, at daybreak or dark, the chief would stand motionless atop the hillock and look out over the long sweep of land that had been home.

So goes the legend. In tiny and wayside Tehuacana, astride its ridges by the little hill, some old-timers may still exist who can tell you the story, if they choose.

The Tawakoni were allies of the eastward, forest-bound Caddos, or Tejas—as Spain knew them. They were an industrious, friendly people who formed a western barrier against the more predatory plains warriors. Before 1800, Philip Nolan, scouting for President Jefferson, lived with them and corralled mustangs near their fine, flowing springs.

By the 1820s, the westward-driven Cherokee felt they held Mexican title here, and this Tawakoni people stood in their way. An indecisive battle was fought within what is now Waco; a second Cherokee strike caught the Tawakoni hopelessly off guard, burned to the ground their hillside, beehive-shaped dwellings, and virtually annihilated all within them. The few who escaped carried with them the chieftain's son. They believed the boy would live to lead the Tawakoni back. The father died in Cherokee flames.

That last stand would go into the record years later, from the memory of an Indian scout for Earl Van Dorn's Second Cavalry campaigning far to the west, on the Washita River. To troopers, the scout was simply Tawakoni Jim, but seared in his memory was his father's death on that distant, flaming hilltop.

As stories do, this one drifted back over time, and Tehuacana settlers, against first or last light, claimed to glimpse the hilltop sentinel. They were sure of what they saw—a father waiting for his son's return.

The story has been borne out by archaeology. Near Barry Springs on Tehuacana's eastern slope, scientists located the ancient village. They traced the sunken floors and their central fire basins, found the lodge pole marks for oval dwellings. They gathered artifacts clearly identified as Tawakoni. Above all, they found a village razed by conflagration.

The childhood memory of cavalry scout Tawakoni Jim was, indeed, fact.

A minister, Reverend J. W. Pearson, would later trace that scout's lineage and authenticate the man. He was the chieftain-to-be, smuggled from his dying village. In the early 1900s, Jim died at age ninety, the return of his people a lost dream.

There are those who believe that the ghost continues to return, even long after his son's death. Some years ago, Robert Carter, who then ran the little village store, relayed some of his family's stories. Daybreak or day's end, take your choice, there was a fair chance to glimpse the statue atop that hill. You had only a glance, though: his appearance was momentary. Approach him, and he would vanish.

I wondered if the old chief had more than one purpose for returning again and again. Could this have been penance for allowing his people to be caught hopelessly unprepared to defend themselves? Could he be there as a symbol of warning?

Around today's village, glancing at the old building that once was Trinity University, I asked if anyone had seen anything up on that hill recently.

In the store, a few glanced up, smiling, and went on with their talk. A young fellow working on his big-wheeled hot rod couldn't understand my question, his radio turned up too loud. On the hilltop itself, a man leaned from his pickup to toss a beer can toward the trash barrel. A ghost? He hoisted a fresh Coors in salute to the ones he believed I must have consumed.

That last visit, I left Tehuacana from that pleasant hilltop shaded with hackberry, a little park overlooking a vast out spill of countryside. I'd never yet seen the hilltop chieftain. Perhaps he had given up returning.

Who'd listen to his warning today? The warning of what happens to a people when they let down their guard?

As I drove away, I thought about that. Just down the hill, I looked back. Something, I felt, had watched me leave. I'm sure what I saw was a tree. Strange, I hadn't noticed it while there. It was about the size and shape of a proud man.

JENNY OF THE MCDOW

Erath County

It is difficult to view this tranquil meadow and envision a ghost that stalked its edging stream for so long, and to such deadly ends: how to reconcile those deaths with once-pretty Jenny Papworth, a happy young wife?

You will find the meadow flanking Green's Creek, east of Dublin and south of Stephenville—a broad vale, gentle with random stands of pecan and oak. Dublin's Wes Miller led me there, guiding upstream a half mile, finally to reach the creek's long and deep-bottomed McDow Hole. From the old wagon-road crossing we had climbed a timbered bank and in a tangle of shinnery, stopped before a great, dead stump.

"That was the hanging tree," Wes Miller told me. "Right near the cabin."

Where it all began, I thought to myself.

"It had a big, long limb parallel to the ground," Wes was saying. "When I was a boy you could still see the ridges—bark grown over rope strands."

Almost half a century previous, a young Wes Miller had plowed that opposite field and sensed that his mules saw Jenny, dead as the baby she carried, somewhere near that stump where we then stood. The compact, quick-striding man, whose eyes never fully released any land that he studied, knew the fabled McDow Hole—and what haunts it—as well as any. More than a century ago, when this story was beginning, his grandfather lived just west, beyond a low rise.

More than once, Wes had sensed Jenny's presence. He had never seen the specter that Jenny became, certainly not as others did, but he seemed to understand why there were those in the nearby towns who would not venture near the McDow Hole. Not after dark.

In bright sunlight, it was easy for me to picture that young wife. She never intended to kill anyone, I had decided, except that vicious neighbor: the others died of fright.

Poking through the brush, Wes broke my thought. He had found the cabin site of Jenny and Charlie Papworth. It was time to consider how it all began.

The Papworths were Georgians who ox-wagoned to Texas in the 1870s. There was a young son, Temple, and a baby yet to come. Beside the McDow, one of Erath County's best water holes, there was the Papworth cabin and, after two hard years, the prospect of a good life. Not too distant were friendly neighbors like the Keiths and McDows. The Comanche shared these lands and were drifting west, and, if cattle rustling had begun to plague other early settlers, the Papworths seemed remotely secure: with the baby, four of them now.

Then grim news came from Georgia: both of the husband's parents had died, and he must leave for a time. Though he worried about a nearby group of outlaws led by a man named Brownlow, Charlie Papworth had a plan for his wife's safety. She could tend household chores by day and spend nights with the Keiths or the McDows. Because he could take a train much of the way, he'd be back before she knew it.

And so the young wife waited, dutifully leaving her lonely cabin each twilight with the children. Then came one night when she appeared at neither the Keith nor McDow homes. In the morning they came searching: there was blood on the floor; Jenny and the baby were gone. Under the rawhide bed, they found Temple, incoherent with fear.

The search broadened and neighbors joined in. Initially, Comanche raiders were accused, but that trail led to a dead end.

By degrees, suspicion fell on Brownlow: his quirt was found near the cabin, but nothing could be proven as witnesses, however disreputable, placed him elsewhere. Gradually the search ended, and the trackless brush lay still. Within it somewhere, the woman and her baby had disappeared.

When Charlie Papworth returned, something within him snapped—plain crazy with grief, neighbors whispered. More than crazy, maybe—he had strapped on his gun to hunt. Man-hunting, some said, for little Temple had told his father just enough: one man had taken his mother, and that man had spoken English.

Feeling himself a target, Brownlow acted—he spoke a word here and there in the right ears. What did anyone know of these Papworths from Georgia? How could they have prospered in just two years unless Charlie Papworth rode the night with Erath rustlers? Who could prove that he'd really gone to Georgia? Why not loose a posse of vigilantes?

And so it seems inevitable that one midnight, young Temple Papworth again awoke to terror. From the cabin, masked men dragged his father, along with six other unknown captive men, to the big pecan tree and hanged them all along that long, straight limb. Frantically, Temple climbed the tree and, one by one, cut those men down. For six, it was too late. But Temple's father lived, and the two of them were able to ride away, westward and out of this story. The story, however, was far from its end, for Jenny Papworth remained.

Surely, psychics will tell you, she witnessed the hanging too. She would have known that a masked Brownlow led those hangmen. What else, then, but an oath of vengeance?

Outwardly now, the Papworth cabin stood empty, a violent place to avoid. Yet there beside it was the finest waterhole in all that rolling country, while drought lay withering on the land. At some point it occurred to Keith that he could save time and labor. Why not move into the vacant cabin? A temporary arrangement, of course, for one day the rains would return.

But the very first night, Keith awoke. Something was at the door. When he opened it, there confronting him stood Jenny, holding her baby. As he stared, she disappeared. Though he barred the door the second night, she walked straight through the log wall. Nightmares, the man tried to tell himself. The third night, his lantern lit, he remained awake. At the door this time, the puddle of lantern light allowed no mistake— he could have touched the woman. He gasped a few words—was it really her . . . well and safe? Her reply was a frightful scream, then empty night. And forevermore afterwards, Keith avoided Jenny's cabin.

An Erath newcomer, however, did not. Down from Pennsylvania, his trade was coffin-making, and he shrugged off the cabin's deaths—that human state was nothing new to him. No, living alone did not disturb him. He had his fiddle, and besides, he enjoyed the solitude.

But when quiet had hovered too long over the McDow Hole—uneasy neighbors claimed they'd not seen the Pennsylvanian for days, and that his fiddle had been silent too—they organized a search. And what did they find but the coffin-maker dead on the floor, his eyes bulging with horror. There seemed little room for doubt: the man had seen death, not in repose, but advancing upon him. It had to have been Jenny. Her cabin must be left alone.

Still, some were drawn to that deserted place, for rumors persisted that the Pennsylvanian had buried money nearby. By daylight an occasional hole was scratched along the creek bank, but eventually two professionals (rumor was they had robbed banks) moved in to the cabin, heeding no warnings, determined to find their due. Not long later, one was found dead on the floor, his face distorted with fright, and the other was never seen again. In Jenny's door was a close-grouped pattern of bullet holes, chest-high and deadly to anything that a revolver could stop.

Over the years, the cabin settled into ruin, and the stories of Jenny roaming the nights continued. There was talk of the sheriff's hired hand who, on his way to visit a friend, had ridden near the old place in darkening twilight, and had encountered Jenny looming up to stop him. Pale and shaken from his escape, he had drawn his pay, quit his job, and ridden off to the west.

Then there was that man and his wife, loading their wagon's water barrels with the sun scarcely down, when they looked up to see Jenny watching from the opposite bank. Straight over the water she came for them, vanishing only when the man whipped his team into careening flight.

And those two boys who dared to fish that hole. They had run and run, only to collapse at the nearest cabin. In broad daylight, they gasped out, Jenny had come out of the water—just rising from it—and had made for them . . . and almost caught them. Put to bed, one remained in shock and died ten days later from some kind of hemorrhage.

In the tiny settlements of Stephenville and Dublin and the country-side scattered between, opinion was divided. Some believed that Jenny was determined to lead someone—anyone—to her lost grave. Others insisted she was on the hunt.

Railroaders new in the county shared the first view. The Cotton Belt had pushed a line across a mile southeast of the hole, and night after night, Jenny stopped its train. What else but stop, the train crews protested? There, dead center in the tracks, she stood with her baby. Just standing there as the train, wheels screeching, crushed by. Always, they stopped too late. And always nothing but empty night lay behind the train after it had passed.

Another who was certain of Jenny's intent must have been Brownlow. Old by then, and soured with more than years, he had long earlier moved far east across the county and lived like a man in hiding. And now came word that he was ill beyond recovery, ill of something that no one could diagnose. Like the man or not, it was time for the bedside watch of extremity, and one who sat with Brownlow would never forget that last night.

In delirium, his muttering suddenly became clear words of terror. "For God's sake, don't let her touch me!" Over the stricken man, the other bent closer. "The blood!" Brownlow was gasping. "Get her away from me!" Instinctively—perhaps at the feel of unnatural cold—the other turned. For an instant only, he saw what stood at the foot of the bed. Jenny had found her quarry. Before death took him in the early hours, Brownlow revived enough to confess. Jenny had recognized him that night as one of the rustlers, so she and the baby had to die. He had buried them in a seep well on the creek bank, and then filled it with rocks. Floods had changed the creek bed so many times as to make it impossible to find the graves. How to guess where floods had finally laid Jenny to rest?

There was one more recent story of a Fort Worth Boy Scout group who tried to camp the McDow Hole quite some years ago. Their scoutmaster was never sure whether they saw or felt something, but they took no chances and left in the night. Since then, the place has been posted against trespass.

EDITOR'S NOTE: *Shinnery* is a word used to describe an area of dense, scrubby trees or undergrowth. In Texas, it is often an area of scrubby, stunted oaks.

FIREBALL ON THE SAN GABRIEL

Thorndale, east of Austin, along the San Gabriel River

Once upon a time, quite some years before the village of Thorndale grew to the south; a man named Snively pitched his lonely cabin near the steeply timbered banks of the San Gabriel River, northeast of today's Austin. His was a hermit's life, and dangerous: he faced a land the Comanche still rightly rode, a wilderness that could hide all manner of renegades. In all, it was a place full of potential deadliness. The occasional wayfarer traveling along Spain's old San Antonio–Nacogdoches road must have wondered what clutched the solitary man to this empty valley.

Snively did not wonder: he was near some old ruins—Spanish, he was sure—and he had stumbled upon the magnet that draws men. He had unearthed treasure. Did he recognize it for the gold- and silver-chased vessels and artifacts from some ancient church? Or did he simply sight the other ruins and contemplate how much more wealth he might yet find—that lure which must always entrap the greedy?

But it turns out that he was not alone in the knowledge that Spanish church riches might have been abandoned there. Out of Mexico, old story insists, rode hard men who knew of the San Gabriel valley. There, they found Snively and his treasure, and they killed him. Then for reasons inexplicable, they buried the treasure again and fled. Over the years, others came back and left in a similar haste, presumably scared off by whatever had scared off Snively's murderers.

On certain dark nights, the light may be seen, searching the rolling fields near the river. Sometimes it is said to be fearfully brilliant.

Most who have studied the story believe that to find the source of that light, we must go back a long time indeed—say, to the mid-1700s, to the walls of Mission Candelaria. Many years ago Hugo Linke, born on the San Gabriel land that his father had farmed before him, told what he knew of the story of the cursed missions. In the mid-1700s, Spain's eastern outposts—around today's Nacogdoches—struggled to hold their ground against French pressure from Louisiana.

There needed to be a way station linking San Antonio to those forlorn outposts, and Spanish priests selected this valley and established Presidio San Xavier, halfway along. Though the troopers disliked lonely duty and objected to the remote post, the priests insisted. They believed this region's Tonkawa Indians must be Christianized.

But they had not reckoned on the man who would command Presidio San Xavier. He was swaggering Captain Felipe Rábago y Terán, and, in addition to detesting this post, he was a dedicated womanizer. He stirred Indian discontent, and then he took out his frustration on those nearer to him. In an inexplicable act, the captain took the wife of one of his own soldiers, Trooper Ceballos. When that unfortunate man protested, the captain chained Ceballos to the wall of his quarters.

Showdown came quickly. The priests confronted the captain, and he only laughed at them. They carried Ceballos to sanctuary within Mission Candelaria, but the captain rode his horse into the very chapel and returned Ceballos to irons.

Blasphemy. San Xavier's priesthood met it head-on, nailing the order of excommunication for Rábago y Terán to the fort gates. Hellfire awaited every trooper within. Frightened, the soldiery returned Ceballos to his chapel sanctuary.

But the captain was not done. In early dark, disguised as Indians, troopers crept to Candelaria's always-open door. In one quick volley they killed Father Juan José de Ganzabal with an arrow through his heart, wounded another priest, and sprawled Ceballos dead from a gunshot.

So it was that on May 11, 1752, Captain Rábago y Terán had added murder to his list of sins.

In the aftermath, panic engulfed the San Xavier establishment. Its
Indians fled. Spring rains, usually falling all about the land, ceased in
this valley. While other rivers ran full, the San Xavier shriveled, rotting
with dead fish. Cattle died. Brambles encrusted the once-splendid fields.
Inside the fort, the soldiers themselves began to fall, struck down by
fever and smallpox. When lifted, their cankered bodies simply came apart.

This was the last report of the last Spanish commandant of the presidio,
the man who had replaced Rábago y Terán. He was sick and dying. He
could see the final terrifying sign—a fierce ball of fire that appeared
over Candelaria night after night. Always it seemed to circle over the
guilty presidio.

Finally, the San Xavier establishment was abandoned, its occupants
retreating closer to San Antonio. What was buried in hasty departure—
Spain's practice oftentimes—was never really known. What is known
is that the fiery manifestation remained. There are those who believe
that its continued return was caused by the incredible disposition of
the guilty captain Rábago y Terán—vice-regal acquittal and a more
important command.

Hugo Linke did not speculate. The San Gabriel valley he farmed
showed no more signs of the desolation once visited upon it, yet he did
not scoff at what happened so long ago. The fireball still comes back, he
explained. Across his south pasture, circling the hill where Candelaria
worshiped, hovering right above the spot where the long-ago presidio
stood.

Is the unearthly light a ghost or a curse, or both? There seems to be
little doubt that something like the plagues of Egypt struck that valley
so many years ago. Whatever it is and whatever it points to, perhaps it's
best to follow Hugo Linke's policy: Leave it alone.

EDITOR'S NOTE: The site of San Xavier was listed in the National Register of Historic Places in 1973. Today there are no traces of the mission and the site is closed to visitors to protect it. There are roadside markers to commemorate San Xavier and other Texas Missions.

The San Antonio Missions National Historic Park is two hours southwest, in San Antonio. It is dedicated to remembering the missions of early Texas. Free tours are available to visitors.

SAINT OLAF'S CONGREGATION

Cranfills Gap

Steve Hagen-Dass recalled hearing voices approaching from the dark outside the church. He couldn't make out many words, for they had seemed unnaturally muffled. But he had sensed a certain anger. And there was no doubt that the voices mounted as the pianist played Hymn 56 beside the altar. Then the voices had drawn to a close. Then the back door of the church pushed open to reveal nothing outside. Nothing but the night.

The tall, soft-spoken man had guided me from his office in nearby Clifton, up the pastoral Bosque valley, northwest of Waco, to the century-and-a-half-old St. Olaf's Church, about sixteen backroad miles west of Cranfills Gap. Built in 1886 by Norwegian settlers, it had served that village until 1917, when those parishioners built closer to town. Since then the old sanctuary has been without a congregation.

We topped a valley rim, and there it waited, austere white-plastered rock, squarely self-sufficient—if alone—on an oak-fringed slope, its modest bell tower lifting against a line of low hills. You could envision its long-ago Lutheran worshipers crossing this valley, summoned by the old bell. Carefully preserved by their descendants, St. Olaf's does seem to await, as long as you come in proper reverence. It also seems to forbid, if you come for other purposes.

So far as anyone knows—or wishes to tell—this story had its beginnings in the fall of 1976, when Fort Worth photographers came down to include the church in a collection of historic buildings. Lee Angel and his son, Mark, were guided that day by a woman we'll call Kate, who knew St. Olaf's history. That day, Kate related that history to one as the other busied his camera.

They seemed promised a pleasant afternoon, a quiet broken only by distant country sounds and the whisper of the camera's shutter. Up ladder-like stairs, Kate had reached the little balcony with Lee Angel when the son put aside his camera below them and went to the piano beside the altar. "Clair de Lune" would relax him, suiting the gentle quiet, he thought.

Then below the balcony they heard the voices, indistinctly muffled, the words an unintelligible garble, but angered. Kate and Lee hurried down to see who was arguing. At the piano, the son had heard nothing.

Now the father played, and, with Kate, the son retreated to the rear of the sanctuary. From beyond the walls, a subdued clamor rose again. All three had heard now, yet not one word could be understood. Intrigued, they returned that night. With the piano's first chord, the outer voices waited to close in.

Several months later, in early 1977, the Angels returned with Jon McConal, a writer from the *Fort Worth Star-Telegram*. They brought a photographer and a tape recorder, and stood in the rear of the church or in the balcony; they all heard the voices, but the recorder didn't pick up anything unusual, and the photographer captured nothing.

McConal later wrote that they thought they heard footsteps. He described the voices as muffled, as though passing through a wall or a blanket of time. And they finally figured out why they hadn't been able to understand the words. The voices, it turns out, spoke in Norwegian.

We had reached the dark-stained altar with its semicircular communion rail. Speaking softly, Steve gestured toward the sanctuary's side windows: there are small, stained glass panels under each arch. "It's beautiful here at

Christmas—cedar boughs in all the windows, candlelight all about. You come in from a cold night, the stove crackling, and the scent of cedar . . ."

He broke off and pointed toward the big stove. "Just in front there is where Kate played the piano when she and her sister brought me out." He supposed he was among the first to come; this church's importance to him was generally known. Each time he came, they played Hymn 56, an old Concordia favorite, and the voices continued to protest.

After a while, it became a bit of a fad to go hear the ghosts at St. Olaf's. There was a particular night in which two carloads, mostly skeptics, arrived. Apparently they were making so much noise that they heard nothing. True believers in the voices find this understandable.

Steve recalled his final visit. Again, Kate and her sister had accompanied him, and again Hymn 56 had roused the voices. This time more than ever. Steve had retreated beneath the balcony.

"Why would it affect them so much?" I asked. "You said it was a favorite hymn."

He tried to explain. "It's 'Oh, Holy Spirit, Grant Us Grace.' I suppose it seemed irreverent, the way it was being played in this sanctuary. Not so much as a hymn. . ."

"But as a lure," I finished his thought.

Steve nodded. "That night I did recognize some Norwegian words. It was very still outside, and the voices grew louder and came closer and closer." He paused. "Then behind the altar, the door opened."

Twice, he explained, he had closed that door, feeling a force from outside. But outside, the night was dead still. Eventually, he had to wedge a chair to hold it closed. After that, they decided not to pursue the ghosts any further. And they removed the piano, bringing it back in only for special services. It felt the most respectful thing to do for those members of St. Olaf's who had in fact, apparently, stayed on at the old church.

EDITOR'S NOTE: St. Olaf's remains a working church, open for many types of services, including weddings and christenings. Locally referred to as the Rock Church, it was designated a landmark by the Texas Historical

Commission in 1974 and added to the National Register of Historical Places in 1983. King Olaf V of Norway also visited the church in 1982 to commemorate the community's ties to Norwegian heritage in the United States.

The church has an active website at rockchurch-gap.com

BELOW THE NORTH PASS

El Paso, Socorro, San Elizario

It has been told that in old Socorro, under the great gateway mountains of El Paso, there remains an ancient adobe where on dark nights one may hear the sound of digging. The digger, of course, seeks treasure; but do not search him out and—as the old and wise can warn you—under no circumstances hunt the wealth yourself.

There has long been a mystique about Texas's mountain-girt, westernmost city of El Paso. So big to be so far apart from others. So high, to be so dwarfed by the peaks about. There is the sense of age there, and of legacies from times long past. Little wonder that it is said to harbor many ghosts. The digger is one of them.

There are others. At old Hart's Mill, beware of the birdsong. It is that of an evil woman who pays for killing her children. Drive the twisting Trans Mountain Road with care: a hooded figure, together with a fierce dog, may spring at you from the night. Be forewarned that the baroque old Plaza Theatre houses apparitions as well, one of them a long-ago Spanish lady who will not leave the site of a garden she once tended.

No one knew El Paso's phantoms better than Dr. Charles L. Sonnichsen (1901-1991). This Texas professor combined the searching mind of the scholar with a writer's deft pen. Many years ago, he related the digger's story—it obviously intrigued him. So did that of another Spanish aristocrat, downriver at neighboring San Elizario.

Suppose we consider them in the order that the road from El Paso comes upon them.

So long ago that it was common to dress in either leather or velvet, and to carry a sword and jackboots, a Spanish gentleman arrived from Mexico in the village of old Socorro, midway on the road to Santa Fe. Being obviously of the Spanish aristocracy—he was handsome, urbane, and impeccably courteous, but aloof—his choice of a humble adobe home confused his new neighbors. Who was this man and what was he doing in Socorro?

Of course, there were theories. Some said he had a daughter and often wrote to her. Others spoke of a map in his possession. But why had he selected such a humble dwelling place? What did he do there? With discreet intensity, Socorro watched him.

By day he went his way in withdrawn gentility. But by night, unquestionably from that dark dwelling came the muffled sound of digging. Perhaps one might approach closely enough to look within. One resolute woman attempted this endeavor, and she fled in horror. The digging she indeed had heard, then something else, something fearful—the sound of desperate, despairing struggle.

In the morning, they found the Spanish gentleman dead in the deep hole that truly he had achieved. On the rough table beside was an unfinished letter to his faraway daughter: he was so close to the wealth that his map promised! His map? Had someone taken it? It was nowhere to be found.

Even after the Spaniard was buried, Socorrans claimed to hear the sound of digging from within that dwelling.

I made inquiries at the old mission as well as at a nearby cantina. Was the man's adobe known? Did he still dig?

"Who knows?" A smile. A shrug. An occasional gesture of tolerance for the curiosity of a stranger. Who knows? They know—the old ones do. They know, also, that you leave such things alone.

I went on downriver after that, to find out more about a neighboring ghost, one I'd heard about in San Elizario.

Beyond the road bend lies its plaza, sleepy and little-changed for some three centuries, its white mission church, its old *carcel* and what was once a many-room adobe mansion. It is this crumbling adobe whose many rooms concern us. Long, long ago it housed a dry-goods business and many a plotting politician in the 1870s. It was the opulent home of Don Mauro Lujan. For more than a century now, his specter has wandered about these rooms.

In his lifetime, Don Mauro was a man of presence and power, a leader in the village's struggle for control of El Paso County, indeed a caballero, a jefe in every sense.

Still, as it must for all, age whitened his hair and bent his carriage, then death came for Don Mauro. Yet those of San Elizario, so long accustomed to the dominant will of this gentleman, were to learn that he did not so easily leave his home. Later tenants told of a white-bearded grandee who wandered nightly from room to room.

Dr. Sonnichsen tells of Maria and Alejo de Ramirez, who lived in that home at one time. A bold woman, Maria was determined to stand her ground with the old gentleman ghost. Why did he continue to pace the rooms they occupied? What did he want from them?

Now it is known among the *viejos* that a ghost, particularly one of quality, will not speak unless addressed directly. And so it was that Maria de Ramirez was first to learn of the treasure known to Don Mauro. Now buried, of course, it could yet provide masses for his soul, pardon his past sins, and leave enough to reward Maria and her husband for their good deeds. Apparently, he led her to the secreted silver.

It was then that greed overtook Maria de Ramirez; she and her husband crossed the river and, with their new wealth, opened a Ciudad Juarez store. But her plan to get away from Don Mauro proved ill-conceived, as Maria became immediately ill and died soon after, leaving the business to fail, and her husband to disappear from this story.

In time, an elderly couple moved into the aging mansion: Bonifacia and Antonio de Maciel. They knew nothing of the dwelling's past, or of its landlord, but seemed to show a certain adaptability that age had bestowed upon them. It seems that Bonifacia was not one to be frightened by an apparition.

Her husband, Antonio, worked late into each night, and it was in those dark hours that Don Mauro chose to revisit his home. How often the visitations occurred within the Maciel household, we can only guess. Still, it is known that Bonifacia, however warm her heart, finally felt compelled to speak with a friend.

What was known of the old gentleman who walked about the house by night? It did not surprise her to learn that Don Mauro had been one accustomed to command. Indeed, very little concerning that gentleman seemed to confound the elderly lady.

No, he did not speak of treasure. Bonifacia paused momentarily, then with her friend, confided. "For much of the night, you know, I am alone," she blushed. "He gets into bed with me."

Surely, the friend gasped, when Antonio came home, the specter disappeared?

On the contrary, Bonifacia's husband could not lie down without permission. *"Con su permiso,"* was Antonio's only passport to rest. And the old gentleman? He merely moved over!

Knowingly, the friend nodded understanding. "Don Mauro is said always to have liked the ladies."

"Yes." Bonifacia agreed, perhaps with the wisdom and enthusiasm of experience. "I know."

THE MOUNTAIN LIGHTS

Marfa, Alpine, Presidio

Y ou may be one of the many who have seen them more clearly than I. Only once in our western mountains near high-perched Marfa have I thought I glimpsed them—solitary lights far south against the dark and jagged loom of the Chinati Range.

You will note that I refer to "them," for this single pale orb may divide itself into several lights of varying colors that dart about and taunt, and disappear upon attempted approach. They are the baffling Marfa Lights, an unsolved riddle that has mystified thousands for more than a century.

Are they explicable natural phenomena? Extraterrestrial beings, or way markers? Are they of the spirit world? Are they friendly or hostile? Take your choice. There are multiple theories, though no solution here.

No, not a solid solution. Yet I know of one man—and only one— who was confronted by them by their choice. Years ago he was a rancher, near old Shafter in the Chinatis.

He climbed after strayed stock, and a sudden blizzard caught him high in those mountains. Night closed in on him, and even then he could have felt his way along a homeward trail, but not now, not in this freezing gray-black horror. He stumbled through the rim rock, a new chill besetting him—fear of cold that could kill him as he walked, fear of the whistling dark that could conceal a precipice. An outcrop loomed ahead, and he knew he must round it. He could not have known that he was about to leave the makings of a most intriguing legend.

But let's abandon him in the high dark for a moment, and turn to the lights. They have many names—Smugglers's Light, Alsate's Light, the Alpine phantom, the ghost lights, and—to veteran observers—simply "they." They have been pursued, explained away, and ignored by thousands. Since their first recorded sighting by Robert Ellison, pioneering in the 1880s, they have been approached near enough to photograph only once, to my knowledge.

One hundred years after Ellison's time, the *Houston Chronicle*'s Stan Redding and photographer Carlos Antonio Rios came upon the lights, dancing the high blackbrush flats east of Marfa at Paisano Pass. For Rios's pictures, these two came as close to the lights as any, aside from the lost rancher. Redding was to leave the best description, close up, yet on record. This was January 1980.

He said they darted about the ground—red, white and blue orbs, baseball sized. That they blended into one, and then separated. One would zoom high into the air, then plummet down to disappear in the brush, only to pop up an instant later and spin away crazily. Unsupported and unattached, each illuminated the brush over which it hovered. They seemed to know they were on camera.

You can duplicate the newsmen's vantage point, nine miles east of Marfa at the old air base. Look south. The lights roam the Chinati Mountains there, sometimes descending to flirt about the great expanse of flats below. They range far and wide, and have been sighted in the Dead Horse Mountains of Brewster County, from Twin Peaks near Alpine, across to the old mountains near Presidio. And although it was more than a century ago when Ellison first wrote of having seen them, many believe that the lights have been there longer than man's memory.

There are other points of view. They are imagination, one rancher told me. Foxfire, a professor explained. Possible way markers, a psychic suggested—listening/viewing buoys for extraterrestrial beings.

At Sul Ross State University in Alpine, Professor Elton Miles, a lorist and a careful writer, probably conducted the most extensive research yet focused on the lights. He neither accepted nor discounted; he recorded. Miles tells of Robert Ellison wagoning his wife into the emptiness of that mountain country. The two saw what they thought to be Apache watch fires, and then learned that all who had come before them knew better—they had always been there. When later "experts" explained them as automobile headlight reflections, a then-aging Ellison observed that there were "damned few lights, roads, or cars" at that time.

After Ellison, reports increased. Vaqueros saw spirits. World War I observers envisioned guide lights for invasion from the south, as did World War II training pilots, who buzzed the lights. Investigations proceeded—Army, Air Force, surveyor teams, reporters from virtually every major Southwest news medium. Results varied little from the experience of a Major Davidson, back in wartime's early 1940s.

Night after night, Davidson sent an echelon of four planes into the mountains. Ahead of them, the lights fled toward Mexico, then winked out. There was talk of an Army search team—with scientists along—that came too close and was destroyed. Fritz Kahl of Alpine, who flew early missions, pursued the lights into the very jaws of the southern mountains, bombing them with bags of flour—source-markers. Invariably, morning brought nothing but white dust on empty land. Finally the Pentagon issued a terse directive—leave the lights alone.

In the past forty years, those searching the lights increased in number, and so have the legends they left. Most have been disproved. Sul Ross students talked awhile of the lights luring head-on crashes along US 90, though the record does not bear this out. One account recalled a car pursued at speeds exceeding 100 mph, its bumper badly burned. Again, there was no verification. Even the annihilated Army search team was discounted by Miles's research. A McCamey man claimed those searchers were friends of his, fortified by sufficient beer, who stole a base jeep and set out on a private quest, only to wreck the vehicle. Afterwards, to cover the truth, they set it afire, stole back to base, and left the artifacts of legend.

Yet, several decades ago, one surveyor recounted his experiences. His crew was camped in a canyon east of Presidio—a well-equipped lodge. With nightfall, one of his crew visited the outhouse, leaving the door slightly ajar. Through the door came the light, and out the back ran the crewman. That soon, the light had disappeared.

Some viewers cite the spirit world, saying the lights are ghosts. Perhaps that of Alsate, the Apache chieftain. Perhaps those of long-ago miners trapped in a cave-in. Perhaps the phantom campfire of a wagon train massacre.

Still others, largely those long acquainted with the land, insist the lights are not only harmless but also friendly. Joe Bunton, who sheriffed the country from 1926 to the 1940s, saw them nightly: to him, they were old friends. The Lee Plumbleys of Marfa—her father was Robert Ellison—agreed they meant no harm.

Naturally there are "scientific" explanations—reflections from mica deposits, gases, uranium lodes, ordinary phosphorescence, static electricity. But such write-offs in no way satisfy the hundreds who still track the elusive things. One El Paso reporter engineered a ground-air search, all linked to central triangulation and communication. The lights, as always, eluded.

And this returns us to the only viewer—to my knowledge—who has come closer than Redding and Rios. Some years ago, Mrs. W. T. Giddens of Sundown—she grew up in the Chinatis near Shafter—told me of her father's experience. It was he whom we left, high and lost in the night blizzard, facing an immense outcrop barring his way. He felt his way around, and the lights confronted him, flashing much as newsman Redding saw them. Then they "spoke."

They "said" to him—he never could explain how—that he was three miles south of Chinati Peak, way off the trail in the wrong direction, and close to a precipice. He must follow them or he would surely die.

With death by freezing an alternative, he followed those lights to a small cave. There was enough sheltered warmth—perhaps the light gave it—to survive the night. The largest light remained in the cave with him, close beside.

These were spirits from elsewhere and long ago, the man was told. They wished to save him; he could sleep now. With morning, both they and the blizzard were gone, and the man could confirm that they had saved him. For beyond the outcrop where they had confronted him was sheer cliff. And indeed, he was off the trail, three miles south of Chinati Peak.

His daughter accepted this story. "The lights came down in our pasture all the time," she concluded. "They're curious and want to investigate things new to them, like the air base during the war. They're friendly. Our animals had no fear of them at all."

And so—as you see—you may take your choice of explanations. It does seem strange that no thorough scientific probe has ever been undertaken. Is it possible such a probe would simply be kept unreported? For me, it leaves one certainty. In our lonely western mountains, *they* are most definitely there. And of what nature, or for what reason, we may never know.

EDITOR's NOTE: The popularity of the lights has led to the creation of an "official" viewing area as well as an annual festival with a parade and craft fair.

There have been two recent scientific studies on the lights: In 2004, a group of students from the University of Texas at Dallas spent four days recording and testing various theories of the lights. They came to the conclusion that all of the lights they observed were in reality car headlights from nearby US Highway 67. The conclusion was reached by driving along the highway as observers watched from the nearby viewing area. Similarly, in May 2008, scientists from Texas State University used spectroscopic equipment to observe lights for 20 days. They reached the same conclusions as their colleagues from TSU Dallas. This hardly explains, however, what Robert Ellison might have seen in the 1880s

TERROR'S LAKE

Carrizo Springs

The place was cursed long ago with a name—Espantosa, Lake of Terror—for good reason. Beginning in the mid-1800s it seems that most anyone who happened upon this small, jungle-like lake, surrounded as it was with a dark and matted growth, came to regret it. So much so that Espantosa grew in its macabre fame. In 1896, the St. Louis *Globe Democrat* carried a long feature article relating its murderous record. Others, as far distant as New Haven's *Evening Register*, recounted the story as well. The lake, by whatever means, was itself the killer.

It was first noted on a lengthening October twilight, as a small train of *carretas*—boxlike vehicles without tops and with solid wood wheels— creaked its way for camp beside that shadowed lake.

How remarkable, the wagon chief thought, to encounter such excellent timber, such a respectable body of water in this land that had seemed all desert since they left the Rio Bravo. For a moment he halted his wagons. A listless gloom enveloped those trees, and there was a leaden glint to the lake's still surface, but the man chose to ignore his intuition.

And so they made camp. They were bound for the new settlement of San Antonio, and had left the great Presidio San Juan Bautista only two mornings earlier. (The ruins of that presidio, the then-gateway to this province of Tejas, still rest across the river just below Eagle Pass). Their plan was to reach the promising Villa of St. Anthony in ten days. As the men brought in firewood, one observed that it was strange that not one person at the presidio had spoken of this campground. Hadn't the fort guarded this road for fifty years?

Just then a woman looked up sharply, wondering where was the young girl they had sent for water?

It was then that they heard the scream—that of one whom death has clutched with quick terror. There was another, one of horror, from a wagon nearest the darkening lake. A man and his wife came running.

"A monster!" the woman gasped. "It dragged her into the lake!"

"A *lagarto*?" The wagon chief asked, for he had seen alligators in the Rio Bravo.

"Bigger!" The man's voice broke. "In that dark it seemed big as a house!"

This is the story tiny San Antonio would learn when the toiling travelers arrived. Through that night they had seen terrible ghosts rise from black water, ghosts forcing them to withdraw from the frightening trees. They had then given the place that name—Espantosa.

In time, their tale reached San Juan Bautista, where the old and wise ones shook their heads knowingly. Had they not known that an early handful of dragoons, guards for a Tejas-bound paywagon, had been butchered along that road? Had they not heard that those men had thrown their sacks of silver into some lake before dying? Those back at the presidio guessed that it must have been those phantoms rising from the water, and they agreed with the lake's name—Espantosa!

Still, memory is fragile and, unfortunately, often of short duration. The years turned, and *carreteros*, smiling at the foolishness of legend, once more camped this lake. At first glance, it seemed notable only in the flora that surrounded it. Such bounty in this monotony of arid land.

Toward the end of the century, one train arrived late on a moonless night, its drivers having pushed for two days to reach water and wood. They slept a weary sleep in their wagons, for the night was calm. And yet, in the small, dark hours came the thunderclap and blinding flash as the ground opened, swallowing wagons and oxen whole. One poor man survived, half-crazed to tell of their choking cries as the bog closed in upon them. The accursed lake took them all.

Still, some ignored warning of what awaited there.

In 1834, an Englishman named John Charles Beales settled his Mexican grant along the Rio Grande, west of the lake. His settlement, Dolores—some fifty-nine colonists in all—was ill-starred. Drought and Natives of that land, as well as Santa Anna marching north, caused the settlement to shrivel and despair, its colonists trickling away. The last to leave—eleven men, two women, and three children—fled along the Old Presidio Road for San Antonio. They had stopped for the night beside a small lake, surprisingly timbered and verdant for this inhospitable land.

It was there, that night, when the Comanche fell upon them. Every man died, and the children were carried away. This is the story that the two women, later ransomed at Santa Fe, told their rescuers. They could never forget that frightful lake, the lake that was clearly Espantosa.

Toward the late 1800s, two peace officers trailed a wanted man into Espantosa's foreboding timber and died in ambush. Not long after, in 1876, grim-faced rangers flushed the hideout, and hanged the bandits in a row of west bank trees.

So, you see, there are many potential ghosts along that shore.

With a little diligence, you can find the place. Northeast of Carrizo Springs, toward Crystal City, it lies hidden just off Farm Road 1433, back in the lush greens that have converted this former desert to garden. The lake waits, dark and torpid, passive with age, its narrow water slack.

There is a small silted dam at its foot, and two fishing camps on the west bank. Beside the dam, a granite marker tells some of this story and, above that, preserves its name from long ago.

There are two ways to know more. One is to go to the nearby towns. Go to them you must, for it is certain that those who truly can add to this story are not likely to visit the lake with you.

I almost hesitate to suggest the other way, for it is firsthand, in the small, dark hours of the night.

THE LINE RIDER

Tilden, Charlotte

The old fence line and its ranch, one of the earliest so protected, are gone now. The little hill with the graveyard, where the fence followed the creek, is a lonely tangle of brush, and the tiny frame schoolhouse has long since faded away. Even the site is hard to reach. It used to be that you could manage a dirt road up along San Miguel Creek, where it crossed Texas 16 above Tilden. Now it's easier to go down by way of Charlotte, south over rough, corduroyed gravel.

It is unlikely, though, that you'd see the phantom fence rider now. If you had ridden up over a century ago when the brasada south of San Antonio was outlaw country, that would have been a different story. Suppose we follow a vaquero that folklorist Henry Yelvington called Juan Piedra. Juan is about to see the rider, and for him, one time will be enough.

The vaquero had trailed over from old Oakville, southeastward, to see about some cows and, as occasionally it does in this arid country, a sudden downpour caught him. He reined up where the San Miguel is joined by the Leguanillas, a deep-cut bottom thick in timber and shinnery.

Early dark rode with the storm, and although Juan had no liking for a camp by the graveyard, the sagging schoolhouse offered his only shelter, and he took it. For him, rest would be fitful: in the lightning flashes those tumbled gravestones turned to sudden, stark forms. Still, he rolled in his poncho and waited out the night, hoping morning would bring sunshine.

Instead, morning brought sullen gloom and unrelenting rain; Juan held to his shelter, making do on jerky and the last of his coffee.

By midmorning he was startled by the loom of a rider trailing along the fence. The horseman, astride a big bay, wore a broad-brimmed black hat, pulled low. Juan could not make out his face, for the man stared fixedly at the ground. He wore a long black coat over his chaps, and it crossed the vaquero's mind that only a fool would ride in such rain without the protection of his poncho.

He called out to the man; he would share his shelter.

Even with the rain and rolling thunder, the man could have heard him. He was passing close by, edging along the hill where the tombstones huddled, across from Juan's doorway.

Again Juan called, louder this time, but the rider did not look up; it was as though he rode paralyzed in his saddle. He was riding line, all right, but what was wrong with a man who would not acknowledge a friendly greeting?

"What the hell, compadre?" Juan shouted at him. "Come in out of the rain!"

It was then that the vaquero realized that this man's passage was entirely without sound. No hoofbeat, no creak of saddle leather, nothing. And never a glance where Juan stood drenched in the open doorway. The vaquero found his own hand at his holster, but the horseman was drawing away.

Down the slope he rode and on beyond, along the fence, until he became little more than a shapeless form gradually fading into the rain.

Muttering at gringos stupid enough to so drench themselves, Juan deliberately put down the uneasiness stealing upon him. He returned to what was left of his breakfast; he would forget the horseman and dwell on his own wisdom in waiting out the rain. As for the cows, let them bide their time.

But he was not to forget the line rider. Scarcely an hour had passed when the black-clad stranger rode back, slowly and deliberately as before. Still watching only the ground. Had he not found the downed fence? Had he not repaired it? Was it not time now to dry himself?

This time though, the vaquero could not make himself call a greeting. This time his hand went deliberately to his gun butt, yet even as he watched from the doorway, the rider turned from the fence, veering directly past the little graveyard toward the far edge of the hill. Then he was below the hill and lost to Juan's sight.

For what seemed a long time, Juan stared beyond the rim of the hill, where he knew there was no fence and no ranch house, but the black-garbed rider did not reappear, even in the distance. Then he realized, as his eyes searched, that the rain had stopped. For a moment he thought to walk through the gravestones and look beyond the hill, but something warned him to leave that place, and so he saddled hurriedly.

Within an hour, he had reached the ranch house, where the foreman and several hands stood on the porch looking approvingly over their rain-drenched range.

"What the hell kind of crazy fence rider works for you?" Juan asked, the words more abrupt than he had intended. The bad, wet night had made him edgy, he told himself.

The foreman's eyes narrowed. "Where did you see him?"

Juan explained where, and the fact that the line rider had seemed deaf.

"Which way did he ride?" The other's voice edged.

Again, Juan answered, and then explained how the rider had returned within one hour.

The foreman swept a gesture toward the other hands, already on their feet. "Get your guns, boys," he snapped, and then, that quickly, they were all out of the corral, riding hard in the direction of Juan's hill.

Before sundown, they were back, herding three rustlers, their hands tied to their saddle horns. They had buried two others and pastured more than a hundred head that the outlaws had tried to drive off. These three were making their last ride, and it would end at the hanging tree in Oakville.

"You saw our fence rider, all right," the foreman told Juan. "He was a damned good one, too; he always had a feel for when there'd been fence cutting."

He gestured in explanation. "All we had to know was which direction he rode and how long before he got back. Then it was easy to pick up their tracks."

Juan Piedra stared at the man, wanting more explanation.

"He's dead," the other said matter-of-factly. "Ten years now. He jumped some rustlers, too many of them. He's buried under that hill where you stayed. The way he'd have wanted it."

Slowly, Juan shook his head. It seemed he was waiting even more.

"Every time our fences are cut," the foreman continued, "he rides the line until he finds where. Then he goes back to his hillside. Just the way you saw him. Comprende?"

The vaquero only nodded. It was clear he wanted to take his cows and get out of there. And, of course that is what he did, and quite safely, for he lived to tell this story. Few believed him, but that was of little importance to one who had seen such a thing as he had. Were you to try now, in this twenty-first century, to make camp in the tangle along the old Leguanillas road, near the spot where the graveyard and the school lie long hidden, I doubt the black-clad rider would disturb your night. Who has need of his solitary help anymore?

EDITOR'S NOTE: See note on *shinnery*, page 52.

THE THING IN OTTINE SWAMP

Luling, Gonzales, Palmetto State Park

When night closes in on the Ottine Swamp, a strange region of near-impenetrable thicket and bog along some ten thousand acres that flank the San Marcos River below Luling, something goes wrong with the evaluation of everyday life forms. As close as I can tell, the thing resembles the "damned thing" in Ambrose Bierce's masterpiece short story by the same name: the monster that lets you see only its movement until it chooses a terrifying visibility.

Something no one can quite describe is abroad in that small jungle. To understand this, consider Berthold Jackson, an A&M engineering graduate and a woodsman who knew the Ottine Swamp as well as you know your backyard. A strong-faced, resolute man, he stalked that creature for more than thirty years as he lived beside the swamp. As with countless other night hunters and fishermen, Berthold found it, most often, stalking him at close range.

From his comfortable brick home on a knoll just south of Ottine, Bertold described one such stalking with his friend, Johnny Boehm of Gonzales, and their dogs. They had followed the soft carbide lights of head mounts through that jungle as the dogs had run loose ahead.

"Johnny was behind me, maybe fifty yards," he said. "I could see his light, and he could see mine. The damned thing got right between us. We could see the brush move." He gestured the rippling movement of passage. "We could hear brush snap underfoot. But we couldn't see a thing, except that brush moving. Not the thing itself. And that close, an animal's eyes would show like headlights."

"You've never actually seen it?" I asked.

"Just its movement. And I've put a big light on it; so have others, more than once. But nothing." He thought awhile. "I've read its track—like a small woman's hand except it comes to a point at the base of the palm, and there's just a stump where the thumb ought to be. I've heard it. Something between human and animal—like nothing you've ever heard in your life."

Steeped as he is in the ways of forest things, Berthold placed this creature's weight at well over a hundred pounds. "Yet," he added, "we've doubled back and seen limbs it stepped on and broke." He shook his head. "So it could weigh more—like an ape."

"When you heard it . . . ," I began.

"We went in after it," he said, pointing toward the woods east of the Warm Springs Rehabilitation Center in Gonzales. "Black dark in there; it moved too fast. We heard it dead ahead, then all at once, a quarter mile north."

I must have looked skeptical, for Berthold Jackson began to name more than a dozen substantial citizens in Luling or Gonzales who had encountered the thing at close range. He claimed that O. J. Behrendt, then maintenance engineer at the center, knew it was his neighbor.

"Billy Webb and Buddy Brown," Berthold recalled, "and Ab Ussery. Talk to them. They're in Luling. They were running a trotline one night, planned to camp there. The thing came along the bank. They could see those bloodweeds moving as it followed them. They were so scared they tried to walk on water."

Needless to say, those three forgot all about camping that night.

Later, I tried to tie in a legend of long-ago Indians pursued by Spaniards. Both were known to have left the trail, and the bog supposedly had gotten them. Maybe this thing was related to their phantoms?

Berthold shook his head. "Mud boils got 'em," he said. "Big around as a room and no bottom at fifty feet. They used to be all over, but they're drying up now. Anyhow, this thing is no ghost."

"What else could it be?" I asked.

Berthold paused. "We call it the Thing."

I kept thinking of Ambrose Bierce. What would the Thing look like if it showed?

Berthold went on to recall a number of other people who'd witnessed it. Brewster Short, Wayne Hodges, their dogs, his own cousin, Lamar Ryan.

But his last experience with whatever stalks that swamp had been six years previous. Differentiating carefully between what he knew firsthand and what he'd heard, he told the story of some folks who had moved into a trailer house, near where he'd seen the Thing's tracks. The people had told him that once or twice something had shaken that trailer like a box. And that the wife thought she'd seen something—something not too big, more like the size of a boy—with the face of some kind of animal she'd never seen before.

Driving away from my camp at Palmetto State Park, itself within the fringe of Ottine Swamp, I thought it necessary to reassure you who may find it as pretty a camp as I have, many, many times. The campsites are on solid ground, and the swamp lies out beyond. The record shows no quiet camper's ever been troubled in that park. And certainly you would be smart enough to restrain yourself from venturing into that surrounding jungle after midnight, right?

EDITOR'S NOTE: The original Warm Springs Rehabilitation Center in Gonzales closed in 2001 after sixty-four years specializing in treating polio and other illnesses.

GHOSTY BRANCH

Glendale, Thornton

What stalks those deep woods can be guessed at from the old stories, handed as they are from generation to generation. In the Confederacy's day, these forests not only hid men escaping a war, they concealed gold whose owners distrusted Confederate paper.

Somewhere near that crossing of Ghosty Branch—the road's been there that long—two men cached considerable gold. They were followed and murdered—the story claims their killers were apprehended, but neither their two bodies, nor their gold, was ever found.

Whether their ghosts would lead you to their graves or their gold, no one is certain. Their behavior is totally unpredictable, and it is possible that both ghosts are there: one seeking discovery, the other vengeance. And how to know which of them you will face?

The sightings began about one hundred years ago . . .

The church meeting had been a long one, and bleak October twilight gathered darkness close about this woodland as the Smith wagon—nine of the family jostling along within it—rounded the bend and made for the old bridge.

The bridge was a creaky wooden affair, a small and nondescript bridge, its creek pressed narrow by the close-crowding pine forest. It must always have been there, young Eddie Smith thought—and he didn't like to cross it, not after dark. It had been there before his grandfather got their place, up the hill beyond and across from the little cemetery. Eddie knew what waited back in those trees along the branch—all his family did. Still, to get home, it had to be crossed and—he drew a deep breath—here it was.

"Merciful God!" someone in the wagon gasped, and Eddie turned cold.

The thing—big, formless, and yet somehow man-shaped—was there, rising from the ground by the edge of the dark pines, blocking their way. There it waited.

Eddie's father shouted something, loud as the crack of his whip that sent the wagon lurching forward. Already, Roy Holland, the hired hand, had leaped clear, levering his rifle, rushing ahead of the team. Almost point-blank, he now emptied that rifle.

But he might as well have fired into the night sky, for the thing turned away and glided up the creek bank perhaps fifty feet. All of them could see the big stump where it paused for a moment, then disappeared. It had not faded into the trees; it had vanished.

The wagon cleared the bridge and careened up the hill, Roy hanging on behind. The rifle had been an automatic reaction with him, but he had known it wouldn't stop that being. Like many in the forests out from old Trinity, he had met it before. The thing had stalked Ghosty Branch for as long as any of them could remember.

That story was recounted by the then-elderly Samuel Edward Smith in his comfortable San Antonio home in the late 1970s. The last time he had known of a sighting was a couple of years previous when the thing had jumped some men hauling hay, right at that crossing. Their truck stalled, and they left it and ran two miles to the main road. Since Ghosty Branch had wandered across his family land for three generations, Smith knew perhaps as much of what haunted that crossing as anyone then alive.

"Sometimes it seems to threaten people, to drive them away," he said. "Other times it's as though it wants to lead a man to something near that old stump."

He pondered for a moment. "If I had nerve enough, I'd go up and stick it out. Follow it and see for myself." He shook his head. "Nobody has yet, though. Nobody I know." He gave a wry smile and explained that if I were to go up there and wait long enough, he'd guarantee I'd see it. His smile faded. "And, just like all the others, you'll run."

"My grandfather was a lawman before he turned to farming," Smith said that day. "He was coming home late one evening, and right by the bridge, the thing rose up and grabbed his reins. For a moment—now my granddaddy had plenty of nerve—he let it lead his horse into the trees. But when they neared that stump, it was too much: he jerked loose and used his spurs.

"On the other hand, there was Brother Alfred—he was our preacher, a kind of circuit rider. He saw it every time he crossed Ghosty Branch after sundown. It never bothered him at all."

For that long-ago Eddie Smith's father, the experience was violently different. He and Roy Holland, walking back from a sick friend's home, reached the crossing at nightfall. The thing was waiting then, and this time it attacked. That elder Smith was a brave man, and he fought it with a knife but he might as well have tried to cut his way through smoke. Still, both he and Holland could feel dead cold hands at their throats. They broke and ran.

"My dad had just bought a new hat," Smith explained. "They went back the next morning—there's never any trouble in daylight—and the hat lay there on the bridge, trampled and torn. His coat was in bad shape, too. From then on, he never walked that road by night.

"And my brother, Bennis, of Refugio, has seen it close," Smith said, thinking back. "Even now, I doubt that he'd get out of his car up there."

According to Smith, almost everyone in the nearby village of Glendale knew what waited up Ghosty Branch. Several men had seen it. I could look them up.

I felt no need for further confirmation and, instead, visited with Smith's cousin, I. M. King, who raised Arabian horses near Glendale. I had intended to set my camper in the crossing and wait but—and you will not believe this—I encountered a week of floods, and there was no getting to that road by night. We went up the next morning when it was passable, and King left me by little Thornton Church, a boxlike, iron-roofed sanctuary on the red hill above the branch. So much timber had been cleared, King explained, he didn't believe that the ghost appeared as often as in the past. About the ghost itself, he was noncommittal.

Eastward, the timber indeed is gone, and even the dense pine upstream along the branch is second or third growth; perhaps the old forest has changed too much. Nonetheless, with my Airedale, Casey, and mud boots, I slogged along the faint forest trail upstream as it led into denser woods, past an old house site, and closing in on the headsprings of Ghosty Branch. Our only trouble was with rain and mud. Of course, it was daylight, and more flooding was expected by nightfall. We left before that.

I carried away one conviction. Since the crossing was relatively open, its woods withdrawn eastward, the best place to lie in wait would be farther into the forest, right up at the headsprings. Whatever is in there would need only to lead you downstream, instead of up.

My parting suggestion: do your best to sleep light and, as well, leave your key in the ignition. I'd go so far as to sleep in the driver's seat. One can break camp fast that way.

THE HAUNTINGS OF
SAN PATRICIO

San Patricio

West of Corpus Christi, the rich and busy fields seem to age, to weather into a sense of things and times forgotten. By out-of-the-way routes, you descend a low hill, and, toward the thicketed and sluggish Nueces River, the near-ghost of San Patricio awaits you, drowsing along Farm Road 666.

If you search for history, as most who come here do, begin at the restored Old San Patricio Store or just beyond, where two granite markers foot the base of what once was Constitution Square. The larger marker tells that this village suffered every misery of the Texas Revolution and, in effect, was virtually killed by it. Here, with the annihilation of his advance guard, began the disasters that would overwhelm James Walker Fannin and his Goliad men.

The historian knows he is standing where many died. Those sensitive to things beyond the routines of dates and places may experience quite something else—that warning chill that suggests ghostly ground. It is that, indeed. Here, beside the marker, you are at the epicenter of perhaps the most haunted region in all Texas.

You have descended from Headless Horseman Hill. You have passed the secluded old cemetery where those who fought and died rise by night, still fighting. Across the gravel road where empresario James McGloin's home once stood, a phantom lady in green materializes with appalling regularity, and the specter of a murdered man has been known to appear to his son-in-law. Beyond, in the dark and dense river bottoms, walks the ghost of the first woman ever hanged in Texas.

Or, so go the legends. Most of the fifty families who resolutely hold to this old land knew the stories at one time.

I saw those legends through the eyes of Lonnie Glasscock. First mayor of a village determined on restoration, he was a mid-thirtyish gentleman farmer who knew his town's history. Before James McGloin built his Round Lake home, his earlier dwelling stood on the south side of Constitution Square. It is there that the first of San Patricio's visitants materialized: the Lady in Green, a story told elsewhere in this collection. Also in that house occurred perhaps the most irrefutable visitation of all.

McGloin's empresario partner and father-in-law was John McMullen, certainly a major patron of all Texas's Irish colonists. Shortly after San Jacinto, he sold his holdings to his son-in-law and moved a mercantile business into San Antonio, all the while maintaining the closeness that had grown between the two men.

It was on a bleak January night in 1853, as McGloin sat before his San Patricio fireside, that his thoughts traveled the long, lonely road that separated him from his father-in-law. In that instant he was struck rigid, for standing before him, his shirtfront sodden with blood, was his father-in-law. Horrified, the younger man could neither move nor, for a moment, speak. That close, McMullen stared straight at him, silent as death!

His voice hoarse, McGloin finally gasped, "What do you want, John?" For an instant longer, the specter faced him, mute, and then vanished.

In shaken haste, McGloin saddled for San Antonio. He must go, he told his nephew, Pat McGloin, and then in minute detail, he told what had happened.

Later, in San Antonio, the son-in-law would learn that John McMullen had appeared before him—as an apparition—at the same moment he had been dying, murdered in that distant city on the night of January 21, 1853.

Even with sunlight glinting upon that granite shaft, it is hard to discount what James McGloin saw so long ago. His nephew's corroboration is on record.

The other San Patricio ghosts? In less distinct focus perhaps, they yet roam the stories handed from one generation to another to explain the faint sounds of fighting heard from time to time in that area.

One legend tells of a party of men bound for new land beyond the Nueces River soon after the Mexican War. These men camped in San Patricio for the night, only to be awakened by the muffled din of fighting. In the shadows beyond their dying fire, Santa Anna's troops were locked in combat with Texas frontiersmen. It is possible that these men were later ambushed by the Mexican troops and that they died here, unprepared.

There is also the story of a Spanish paywagon train, ambushed downriver from the San Patricio cemetery, every one of its guards massacred. In the tangle of mesquite and hackberry, could the ghost-fighting not be them, still fighting to live?

Well above the cemetery where the road tops Headless Horseman Hill, a decapitated rider may still gallop from the dark. Lonnie Glasscock knew of two accounts. One was that of a Kentuckian of means, down for a land purchase, who was murdered for the gold he carried. The other was that the ghost was an ordinary horse thief beheaded for rustling. Which one is the spectral rider?

This horseman, only the very old ones had seen. On a great gray horse—at least on one occasion—he came charging directly into a wagon team, passing soundlessly through its traces, its wagon, the terrified occupants, and that wagon's runaway dust.

But by far, the best known of all San Patricio's ghosts is that of Chepita Rodriguez, the stoic woman who died on a rope—quite possibly, many claim, to shield a loved one.

Chepita was the daughter of a Mexican who fought and died for Texas freedom. The girl, destitute in this then-ravaged land, became the common law wife of an outright hard case; that man, after she bore him a son, left her and took the boy.

Before her time, Chepita grew old, eking out a livelihood from the shack she offered as a meager inn for saddle-worn travelers. One who came her way was John Savage, whose saddlebags carried some six hundred dollars in gold and who stayed the night in Chepita's cabin. The starkest account is that, for his gold, she killed him with an ax.

The counterclaim contends that Chepita's lost son returned, and that it was he who killed Savage for his gold. Chepita, having recognized her son as he fled, refused to disclose any information about him. In the courtroom, Chepita declared only that she was innocent.

According to Lonnie Glassock, Chepita was tried and sentenced by an itinerant judge near the time-erased square and the Old San Patricio Store. She rode the death wagon to the riverbank, took her last draw on a cornshuck cigarette, and disdained a blindfold. They buried her by the mesquite tree that hanged her.

"Some say the mesquite died almost immediately," Lonnie Glasscock said. "Some say it was struck by lightning. Every now and then, some traveler will come into the store, white as a sheet—maybe too many beers, who knows?—saying he's just seen Chepita out there in the night. Always in those dense trees down by the bridge where you cross."

Glasscock claimed never to have seen her. Nor did anyone know exactly where the hanging tree stood—so many floods over the years.

"The legend," he said, "is that she appeared whenever a woman was about to be executed." This has grown to a variation—perhaps why so many seek her—that Chepita walks the night whenever any unjust accusation assails any Texas woman.

Over the years a great myth has formed around her. The trial was controversial and widely seen as botched; the documents relating to the case have all vanished; rumors of her being buried alive swarmed in the years following the execution.

Begin your search at the granite markers, regardless of what you seek in San Patricio. And if you'd rather meet only present, living occupants, search by daylight.

EDITOR'S NOTE: In response to the myth, in 1985 the Texas state legislature absolved Chepita of the crime. Despite this, she is said to walk the dry riverbeds around San Patricio to this day, a noose hanging around her neck.

THE FAITHFUL WIFE

The King Ranch, Falfurrias

To encounter the lady, you must drive this road by night. I was below the little towns of Alice and Ben Bolt, in the southward brush. Ahead was the overpass lifting US 281 over Farm Road 141; beyond it, a line of mesquite that marks Escondido Creek sliced the flat sweep of chaparral. It looked like it would have been a good place to stop. How slowly that long-ago little carriage must have jostled this way.

I kept thinking about the girl, her last night alive. I imagined her eyes wide with terror, peering from the little coach at just such an empty night. My thoughts, indeed, rode more with that girl than they searched for the woman I understood I might see, waiting by the road.

Trucks were pounding the highway ahead of and behind me. Too much traffic, I felt. Too many headlights for her to show herself. Over two centuries ago, how terrible the envelopment of darkness would have been for that girl.

The mesquites were big, great clumps of them, where the side road bent east across the upper reaches of the vast King Ranch. I turned and drove that road for a few miles, then came about and went back to my camp. In fact, the woman had not elected to show herself.

I had searched for the Lady in Black, whose story was first published, so far as I know, by Professor John J. Sauvageau. His field at what was

Texas A&I University was linguistics, and he delved into the folklore of South Texas. His trilogy, *Tales That Must Not Die*, is told in both Spanish and English.

Sauvegeau had recalled four men who worked the night-shift at the nearby refinery. At this very intersection, the men had driven straight through a woman who had walked out in front of their car. When they stopped, however, there was no trace of her. Nothing but the quiet night and the opaque wall of mesquite. Others had seen the phantom woman, and Sauvageau investigated. Her story, as shortly you shall learn, goes far back.

It should be noted, however, that many continue to see the Lady in Black. Just before I went down to search for her, my daughter called from Corpus Christi, where some knew the old story. The brother of a fourth-grade teacher, a friend of hers, had driven that road some nights earlier. In the glare of his headlights, the lady was silhouetted against the mesquite by the roadside. He braked, and then backed. Perhaps he could help someone in trouble. But she was neither beside the road, nor in the trees. Nothing was.

To the south from that overpass, where Palo Blanco Creek merges with Arroyo Baluarte, Falfurrias had an upbeat look with its palm-lined downtown brick. However, back in the mid-1700s, Spanish rancheros pushed out from the Rio Grande settlements of colonizer José de Escandón. They ran their broad-horned herds over this spacious land.

One such rancher, Sauvageau related, was Don Raul Ramos—in his substantial hacienda, prominent among his few neighbors. Darkly handsome, he was also considered a catch for any girl, and at least one neighbor's daughter felt that Don Raul would ask for her hand in marriage.

But instead, from interior Mexico, he brought a lovely young girl, Leonora Rodriguez. Doña Leonora would be mistress of the vast Ramos domain. The wedding provided a festival, and the honeymoon a promise of happy times for this couple.

Only one small cloud marred their horizon. Don Raul's affairs called him away, perhaps even so far as a journey to Spain, he told his bride.

No, he would not risk her on such a dangerous voyage. Let her wait and come to know this broad land they would both love. He would be home again before she knew it.

But in fact, he was gone for more than half a year.

He returned to find his wife pregnant. And the baby was not his, whispers told him. Raging, he did not stop to realize that the jealous women who had expected to preside over the Ramos fortune had suggested Doña Leonora's infidelity.

Dress her in black, Don Raul commanded the household women. Then he summoned his vaqueros. They would escort her one day north, while he—for fear he might relent—would saddle and ride the same distance south. At the end of that day's journey, the vaqueros would hang Doña Leonora.

Even today, the land is lonely from Falfurrias northward for a day's travel by horse. It is hard, driving it by night, not to feel the dark that young girl saw closing about her. She was innocent, she had wept before her husband; the child was his, for she had loved him truly.

To those vaqueros, their faces drawn in dust and sweat, she had cried this out. Yet what could a Ramos rider do? The patron was a violent man, and never had they seen his fury greater than this. And the girl? They could not look at that fair, slim throat; they detested their coiled reatas that would knot the noose.

There was nothing to do but push on and on, until the dark hid the face of the girl. Then let sunrise hurry; let them get it over.

Later, they would not recount the hanging. But as always with even the deepest of secret things, it became known that Doña Leonora at last had gathered herself in furious pride. She had made a vow that no Ramos rider would ever forget.

They would see her again. Then, they would know her innocence!

To the south, where the oak mottes of tiny Encino mark a day in the saddle below Falfurrias, Don Raul must have known—some inexplicable transfer of thought—that outburst of truth from his young wife. For it was there, even as the girl hanged, that the ranchero put a pistol to his head.

How Leonora's fidelity came to be acknowledged has been obscured with time. Perhaps a deathbed confession elsewhere, perhaps her immediate appearance by the stand of trees where she died. Today, those knowledgeable of the great brasada and its people from long ago know that the young wife was faithful. She was faithful then; she is faithful now. Why else, in the very black dress that she wore to her death, would she return and return?

"Just recently," a Falfurrias newsman told me, "a truck driver stopped to pick her up. It was like the others: she was there, and then she disappeared. Over in Corpus, they're doing a song about her."

As for me, I could have camped Escondido Creek, although the land is hard and I confess preference for the facilities of Lake Corpus Christi. Anyhow, it wasn't really necessary for her to appear before me, that night I went looking. About lovely Leonora Rodriguez de Ramos, I never entertained one doubt.

Now you may wonder why I didn't drive on to tiny, southward Encino, so that I might peer into the night where the oaks stand back from the road and where Don Raul shot himself. It was not that the comfort of my camp was distant, and the night was growing old. I drove back because I had the answer.

Why would that brutally relentless ranchero wish to show himself?

THE FIDDLER

Brazosport, San Bernard River

This happened, they say, more than a century ago and, at the San Bernard's mouth, near Brazosport and Freeport (once called Velasco) and Surfside, it has been repeated many times since—to those who have dared the haunting of Fiddler's Island.

As the river crept along, slack and dark, its mouth opening secretively into the Gulf, a man rowed his boat slowly into the current, pulling against it just enough to keep station on the point marking the river's end. He took care to dip his oars noiselessly, for he was waiting for the other sound. The "singing river" the San Bernard was called, and if it were true, there must still be treasure buried somewhere about.

What was it that he heard now? Surely, the working of tidal currents against a shell bottom. Yet there was a thinness, a reediness, like the sawing of a fiddle at some forgotten sea chantey. Indeed, from the near dark, he could distinguish some antique tune. Still, he was listening less to its melody than to its volume.

Unquestionably, the sound was swelling.

The man stopped rowing; it was quite loud, clearly that of a fiddle now, an enormous one, and from the black water all about, it seemed to envelop him, threateningly discordant.

It pressed upon him like a wall, something that you could almost reach out and touch, or something that reached out for you. From the bank, observers saw the boatman last when, not waiting to beach his craft, he scrambled out, leaped on his horse, and whipped it away into the night. There had been just enough light to see his face—pale with terror.

In its brief, upper reaches, the San Bernard is a tenuous and inauspicious stream, gathering to full, dark flow only near the old Brazoria coast, a hundred miles from its head. You can reach the mouth by farm roads that follow the river west of the Brazoria-Freeport highway. There are some well-groomed houses as well as cottages in sparse timber, and finally the reedy, open coast and the Gulf beyond.

Just inshore from there, at the long-gone tavern of Henry and Nettie Overbay, I learned of this story. Behind that place is a low, treeless island—Fiddler's Island—and if fishing is your aim, you have reached sheltered moorage. However, it is also the center of old, old haunted ground where something once was hidden and guarded by fearful music that no one—so far as is known—has dared to endure to its end.

The legend varies with the teller. One account remembers colonial days when this coast landed Stephen F. Austin's first colonists. A young musician was to bring his bride home here, but he somehow lost her just hours before their wedding. Grief-stricken, perhaps jilted (the details of what actually happened have been lost), he shut himself away in his cabin. What is clear is that the girl disappeared, leaving a very lonely man. Early travelers could see the faintest light from the island cabin, and from it they could hear the cry of that lonely man's violin. He was never seen again, and time took his cabin. Yet on dark nights, his music remained. For the intruder who insisted on searching about, that music was said to rise in volume until it became overwhelming.

A second version retreats even earlier in time to an 1816 pirate sloop, hurricane-driven to haven here, but crushed in the storm. There was a treasure chest from the Spanish brig, the Santa Rosa, sunk off Matagorda Island. There was a survivor—some say two: one who killed the other, then fled with a crude map of the treasure's grave. In time, a strange recluse appeared and built a shack near the river mouth. He fiddled the nights away with his jug and sea chanteys, and through the days he searched the shifting shoreline. Perhaps hostile eyes watched. Perhaps another pirate. It was told that the man was found on his pallet, head and fiddle split, and everything scoured by a searching ferocity. Into the dark waters went that man's body and, with it, his fiddle.

By the early 1900s, coastal old-timers could remember many who had come to Fiddler's Island. Some came, joking and laughing, just to dare the ghost. Others seemed more intent to row out past the island and beyond it to the mouth, where they would await the windy dark, and see what happened.

Some few, I suspect, intended more. Perhaps the beaching of their boats beyond the bend, then a search of the ground. But always they came back in haste, tight-lipped and pale, and were never seen again. So goes the story.

Now one man must have believed these legends, for many years ago—before the river's lower reaches built up—another recluse turned up near the San Bernard's mouth. He wanted no boat; he managed a shack and kept to himself; few knew anything of him beyond the name he gave them—Sandy. The Overbays knew him best, and therein lies this version.

Of indeterminate age and an obvious loner, still he came up to the tavern, comparatively new then, for something to drink. Once when he may have had too many, he threw a handful of Spanish reales on the counter, and then—as though alarmed with what he had disclosed—he scooped them up, lapsed into silence and left.

Not long after, he was found dead in that shack—natural causes, it was determined. No one found any of the Spanish gold, however, and later it was learned that this Sandy had come from the East coast, that he had been looking for this specific river mouth, and that his bank account back home labeled him a wealthy man.

The music of Fiddler's Island is little spoken of these days. The last account I know of is that of a young boy in the 1970s who persuaded his father to run their fishing boat into the San Bernard. The boy—with his father along to share bravery—wanted to test the ghost music.

"Did you hear it?" I asked him.

"We didn't even look," he said. "It got stormy instead. The wind got higher and higher; it made an awful sound."

The music of Fiddler's Island was little spoken of by the early 1980s, perhaps almost entirely forgotten by now. It remains an unsolved story, one of yesterday's most intriguing legends. Maybe there's nothing left for the fiddler to guard. Maybe that recluse Sandy dared the music to the end and found that treasure. If he hadn't died, no doubt he could have told us.

EDITOR'S NOTE: A *chantey*, or *sea chantey*, is a song sung by sailors in rhythm to their work.

THE COASTAL WATCH

Sabine Pass

With the ruthless pirate Jean Lafitte, history and legend so intertwine as to cloud the place and time where—after finally being driven from Texas—he died. Historic surmise suggests the Yucatan shoreline, about 1826. But legend leads us beyond that lost grave.

Now if we follow legend, we return to the marshy and bayou-laced Texas coast below Beaumont and Port Arthur. We come upon vast, brackish Sabine Lake, fed by both the Neches and the Sabine, and all emptying into the Gulf at the deep and dark-running Sabine Pass.

Here we are close by Lafitte's latter-day haunts, secretive waterways weaving through the Louisiana he had known. We are close perhaps to pirate gold. But closer indeed—old story has insisted this for more than a century—to something that may yet stand dreadful guard.

And so, before I suggest a vantage point for your search, why not consider two accounts that govern my suggestion?

In 1921 while duck hunting, that notable lorist Henry Yelvington went slogging through the lonely reach of reeds and opaque bayous that flank the narrows of Sabine Pass. In one of those still waterways he made out the sunken outline of a low-slung schooner, the fast, rakish type that identified a Lafitte raider. From a grizzled coast dweller, Yelvington learned that the hulk indeed had been Lafitte's. Indians, whose handed-along story he was to learn, had seen it sunk under pursuing fire. Whether its crew went down or fled, they were unsure . . . and so was the coast dweller. However, of something else the Indians had been certain. For many years, the waters remained still, the land empty. Then one day, at the lone tree beside the sunken ship, an incredible figure appeared. The figure was a man Running Snake, the Attacapan chieftain, knew to be Jean Lafitte. Lafitte, the man who Indians far southward claimed to have seen dead and buried.

Yet there he stood, all alone. Running Snake approached and, in terrible shock, saw the figure vanish. After that, only from a distance would any Indian watch.

But watch they did, for the figure returned and stationed himself where the waters hid the long boat. Running Snake's companions were not overly surprised when, eventually, a strange, shadowy boat slid noiselessly up the narrow waterway.

From that boat emerged silent men who, as though directed by their summoner, began to raise chests from the sunken vessel. Mutely they worked, loading their boat, and then, with the dead Lafitte standing in the bow, they left as soundlessly as they had come. Were they flesh and blood? Who would venture near enough to learn?

They started toward the big lake, then disappeared in a mist. After that, no one came again. Running Snake and his men avoided the place as well. But they remembered its story.

The second account is that of three men who may have experienced the sequel to the first. Near the early 1900s, the old *Houston Post* reported the recollections of a resident of the city of Port Neches. He was an old-timer named Marion Meredith, and his memory reached to the days before America's Civil War. Like the very few who trapped and fished this coastline before Spindletop, he knew the tales of Lafitte's treasure, secreted on the reedy shores of Sabine Lake.

Meredith had a friend who knew the lonely marshland even better than he and, more importantly, had come into possession of an old Mexican map. Where the Neches empties into the lake, some miles above

Yelvington's bayou, the map showed a pirate cache. Perhaps Meredith knew of the Indians' phantom boat, for he declined to accompany his friend. With the map, that man set out alone.

It was clear that the map led him to something, because he left his shovel and mattock beside a partially-dug hole. He burst into Meredith's cabin, face blanched and speechless with terror. For the few days he lived, the man remained incoherent. It is assumed he died of fear.

Inexplicably, the map taunted Meredith, for along with a nameless dread, he knew he could find the place. If he was brave, he was also prudent and, goaded as he was by the thought of riches, he finally selected a companion searcher—the one man, to his knowledge, who not only knew these dark backwaters but feared nothing.

Call the man Steele; Meredith declined to name him. Steele agreed to the search and, rowing their canoe, they followed the map. On a shell-bank somewhere near the Neches's mouth, they found the abandoned tools and the dead man's hole. By turns, they began to deepen it, one resting while the other worked.

As Meredith recalled, he almost felt relief when they uncovered the first skeleton; if that had terrified his friend, it certainly was not enough to turn them back. They dug deeper and deeper, and as dark neared, the man in the hole was now hidden to his companion, resting beneath a close by tree. As Meredith rested, believing that any moment now he should hear the mattock strike a heavy treasure chest, what he heard instead was a cry, frantic with terror. Steele came clawing from the hole, his eyes wide with horror.

"For God's sake," he shouted, "Get out of here!"

As fright drove their canoe upstream, neither looked back. Finally Meredith ventured the question. What had the other seen? "Hell itself!" Steele gasped. "Hell, in all its horrors!" He locked himself in stunned silence and bent to his oar. Had something come for him from that pit? He only stared at Meredith, but his eyes spoke for him.

Only once again—years later in Beaumont—would Meredith see the man. "Don't ask me about it," Steele said violently. "But if you value your life, stay away from there."

But eventually, something drove Meredith back to that place, alone. He felt he must bury the skeleton and, without looking down, fill that hole. Yes, he told the *Post*, he could direct anyone there . . . anyone who dared. But he would not go farther than to show them, and then he would leave.

Of course, he's gone now, and this leaves us seeking the vantage point I promised to provide for your search. I drove down to Sabine Pass, its green bankside park with Dick Dowling's heroic monument, its oleanders, the line of Louisiana fringing opposite and the gray sea out beyond. Somewhere inland, where the bayous finger off into the reeds, is Yelvington's waterway, where the hulk may yet rest and where Running Snake saw the phantom boat make for Sabine Lake.

Could that boat have beat northward rather than back to sea? Could it have lodged near the Neches mouth, where Meredith feared to return? Could a phantom Lafitte, in true pirate custom, leave only dead men to guard deep-buried treasure?

Out from Groves or Port Neches, you can find the Old Ferry Road easily enough. Some two miles of rough shell will lead you to that river mouth, a little beyond the sea-worn boat club and close by the rusting shell of a shipyard building and the hulks of old ships, dying at their moorage. From a cane-flanked and wooded point of land, you look out on broad Sabine Lake and know you are near Meredith's shellbank.

Behind you loom the lofty Rainbow Bridge and its newer neighbor, the Veterans Memorial Bridge, that lift the coming and going Port Arthur-Orange highways twenty stories into the air. From where you stand, the cars are a stream of tiny insects on a glistening spider web. It is from up there that you can best comprehend the vastness of this once lonely land. And it is up there that I suggest you find your vantage point. They are both high bridges and, even with traffic, safer than searching the bayous.

THE LIGHT OF BRAGG ROAD

Saratoga, Kountze

Where Saratoga's Big Thicket Museum once stood there is now the Big Thicket Field Research Station, part of the National Park Service's National Preserve. Standing there, you feel as if you've nicked a little of its interior along thin, jungle-walled roads. Perhaps you can sense the stand of little towns resisting the advance of forest; the trucks crouched under mountains of new-cut logs, the lonely clusters of tank batteries where drillers and pipeliners have penetrated. Perhaps, you feel an intruder in this labyrinth.

What could not hide up there? There was the Saratoga old-timer who, within a mile of his home, stayed lost for eight days. There was an old red hotel, burned many years ago, and leaving only a few forlorn concrete steps going nowhere.

On a gloomy night, I glimpsed the apparition sometimes spoken of in these parts. Of the scores of mysterious lights that tantalize the breadth of our country, that which dwells in the depths of this dense thicket is—in my opinion—the most intriguing. Something about the manner in which this phantom light is hunted, witnessed, fled from, or ridiculed harks back to uncalendared time.

An early observer was a Saratoga barber near 1900 when the Big Thicket covered almost everything north of Houston and Beaumont and, mile for mile, matched impenetrability with any American wilderness.

Through the pitch-dark tangle, the barber and a friend were night-running foxes. They were wary of the forest, for they had heard it swallowed men. On that night, not the wilderness itself, but that which rose from it, terrified those two men. Suddenly from a black wall of timber, an unearthly luminescence confronted them. Lantern-sized at first, it swelled and glared, and then came at them. As they ran, it disappeared.

"Nothing held the thing up!" the barber insisted in his shop the next day. "It changed colors and sizes like it was alive. It chased us!" To those who doubted him, the barber shrugged and taunted. "Why don't you go face the thing yourself?"

Many did.

There was George Lillis, a sober, reliable fellow who, traveling by wagon up Bragg Road, swore the thing rushed straight through his panicking horses, landing him in a ditch. And there was Lance Rosier, the respected naturalist who knew that thicket best, and claimed that the thing had chased his nephew into the bad, back reaches.

Largely because of work by Archer Fullingim of Kountze to collect and print the growing legends, there were troops of sightseers streaming into the Big Thicket by the mid-1950s. These hordes wanted to hunt it, to photograph it, to run over it, to shoot it. Later, this lore was collected by Nick Rodes, a Midwestern professor, naturalist, and wildlife manager who ran the old museum for a number of years beginning in 1979.

Among these seekers were some able writers. In the early 1970s, *Houston Post*'s Marge Crumbaker recorded a night encounter. Her party of observers included Alice Griffith of Baytown and Ronnie Foreman, both of whom had seen the light close. Foreman, a virtual student of the apparition, counted a score of sightings—once when it crouched atop his car's hood and, for a few fearful moments, hovered just beyond his windshield. On this occasion, the light came at Marge's party from behind.

In October 1979, Anita Baker came down from the *Fort Worth Star Telegram* and, for an hour with her husband, watched the light taunt them. Small and red at first, it flared brighter before darting away or disappearing to reappear elsewhere. There have no doubt been others.

And what was that phantom? There are many theories . . .

It was the ghost of Civil War deserters, flushed from a flaming forest and shot down in the nearby Kaiser Burnout.

It was Mexican workmen who laid the lumber train rails in 1903 and, for pay—so the story went—drew bullets and burial just off the north end of the nine-mile line.

It was a trainman, decapitated when he fell under the wheels—a phantom still hunting his head. Swampfire, contended others. Foxfire. That sort of thing. To some Thicket dwellers, then and now, it has remained no more than a tall tale.

For a while Nick Rodes and his guides took groups up the Bragg Road on Halloween. Though that doesn't happen anymore, guides at the National Preserve Visitors Center say any park visitor is welcome to walk the road alone.

If you dare, begin not quite two miles above the Big Thicket Field Research Station. The research station is housed where the old museum used to be, just after veering off Texas 105 onto 770. Bragg Road is the narrow, sandy lane that runs like a plumb line straight through the close canyon of towering loblolly pines. Beyond lies the unknown—giant palmettos, hidden hyacinth-fringed ponds and bogs, wild orchid twined with tie-vine and briar—a tangle with names such as Bad Luck Creek and Panther's Den. These are places through which you may have to crawl.

THE GATE

Pawnee, Beeville

In this story I have changed some names because descendant families remain, and they prefer to forget the entire matter. Besides, the gate is gone now, and perhaps for the best. Many South Texas old-timers believed that it led from this world into another dimension.

It was an ordinary-looking ranch gate about a mile northeast of the dusty little town of Pawnee, near Beeville. Just above is the old Pawnee cemetery and, as you look south, the headwaters of Sulphur Creek make a wide sweep around a saucer-like valley. Back in the 1870s there was no town at all, nothing much aside from two ranches—call them the Johnson and the Duff—that met along the creek's timberline.

Above them was the raw guntown of Oakville and not much below except what are now the ghost towns of Gussettville and Lagarto, and beyond that, old San Patricio. This was ranch country where James W. Lancaster held sway, his big family cowboying both spreads.

As I said, Lancaster wasn't his real name, which made no difference to the trouble he was about to bring upon himself. A Smith or Jones, hardheaded and dogged enough to try to subdue this land, might have fared the same.

The trouble began when Lancaster determined to dam a dry arroyo spilling into the Sulphur. His vaqueros, knowledgeable about such things, warned him against digging his fill from that sloping bank: on dark nights, certain lights flickered along it, and such signs meant either buried treasure or the dead, and most likely, both.

That was nonsense to the rancher, and with a slip and brace of mules he cut away and, to his consternation, disinterred the remains of some eleven bodies. Years earlier, the eleven had rustled cattle across South Texas, and a posse had caught up, murdering and burying them on the spot. Of a nature not easily turned aside, Lancaster unceremoniously shoveled them under elsewhere and finished his small dam. Doing so, he must have loosed something beyond mortal comprehension.

After that, he couldn't sleep. All about the ranch house, when dark closed on the small hours, the old man could hear unnatural sounds: a harsh knocking on the wall by his bunk, unmistakable cursing, and finally violent shouts and gunfire. Bad dreams, he told himself.

But his silence was short-lived. As he rode up at dusk one evening, a hard-looking man waited on the porch. When he dismounted to face the stranger, Lancaster found the porch empty. A few nights later, he walked into a back room and found a woman with long hair, a disheveled look about her. He turned to put down his gear, and when he looked around, she too had vanished.

And so he spoke to his wife and his two elder sons. All of this had happened since he dug the fill for that dam. The problem must have arisen from the rancher's indifferent disturbance of the graves. It seemed to have done more, however, than merely to set specters roaming the night. Could it have opened a portal to another dimension, a twilight zone where mortals should not go?

Lancaster descendants with whom I talked hold no firm opinion other than that something went wrong with their pasture gate.

To the east of the house was a fence intersection, one string leading down to the Goliad road, another to the holding pasture, toward the creek. In that pasture, from time to time, the Lancasters cut out cattle for their buyers.

One afternoon, several of the family sat out on the big gallery waiting for the Gulf breeze to cool things. Up the fence line came two riders, Jim Farwell and Trey Blankenship. Farwell rode a big black that always neighed when he neared the barn. However, this time the two cowboys did not come straight for the house, as they usually did, but turned instead at the corner gate, leading down to the pasture. Both passed through, neither one looking once toward their friends on the porch. Then, in one astonishing instant, both riders disappeared. When Lancaster and his sons rushed to the gate, they saw no tracks on the wet ground.

Lancaster walked back to the porch and sat down heavily. "They weren't due till tomorrow," he finally said.

The next day, Farwell and Blankenship did come. Up the fence line and straight for the porch, mounted and dressed precisely as before. When asked where they'd been the previous day, they answered: Where else? Up Gonzales way, where they'd been sent—a long thirty miles from this ranch and its gate.

This rancher had no way to know that the doppelgänger was no uncommon thing in Central Europe—a kind of cloned pre-appearance of an expected arrival, a being often sent to warn. He only knew that something had gone wrong on his ranch. How wrong, he would learn shortly.

Again there were cows in the holding pasture, awaiting their buyers. Early in the afternoon, Buck Patton's rig rattled up the fence line with three men inside.

One of the men dropped off to open the gate, but without stopping for a friendly drink before business talk. And this time on the Lancaster porch, a half dozen cowboys watched. They saw the rig pass through the gate, saw the vaquero close it, climb back into the rig, and then with it and all its occupants, simply vanish. It left nothing to mark its passage, neither ruts nor tracks.

And as you've already guessed, the Patton rig showed up the following day, precisely as before but this time, real.

Where had they been the previous day?

Goliad, of course.

That was more than a century ago. Lancaster's gone now, as are his cowboys. Still, the questions come flooding to those of curious bent. Did they really see those things? Was it a mirage?

I tried to envision where that gate might have been. Perhaps the opening, however invisible, is still there. If it were, old man Lancaster could be just on the other side, waiting to give me the straight of this story.

A GATHERING OF SPECTERS

Bee Caves, Austin

This story is not so much about ghosts as it is about those who communicate with them. Still, it's best to begin with the phantom wagon.

Bruce Marshall recalled the story he'd heard firsthand from his great-granduncle, a man who'd seen the phantom wagon as a child. Driverless, the wagon careened wildly, its team dead-running in unchecked terror. It hammered the black-dark ranch road that led toward Bee Caves, west of Austin in those rough hills. And then it was gone, swallowed by the night.

"He told me he saw it near where the driver was shot, years before," Bruce Marshall reflected. "Quite close to here." From his restored, century-old ranch house and studio, the artist glanced toward the choppy Westlake hills near Austin, dotted now with big homes where long before had sprawled the Eanes-Marshall Ranch, founded by his ancestors in the 1860s.

The phantom wagon driver—named either Burns or Barnes—according to legend was ambushed and shot in 1871 near this spot. But he is not the only ghost here, say parapsychologists who came here to make contact with the spirits. Among the others identified are Bruce's great grandfather, Robert Eanes; his grandmother, Viola Eanes; and Hudson Marshall, his grandfather. Perhaps there are others.

"The psychics seemed to regard this ranch house as a sort of ghost hotel," explained Bruce, who looked about his two-level studio and shrugged. "Well, if the ghosts are here, they don't bother me."

When, just after the Civil War, Robert Eanes bought the several-thousand-acre ranch from his brother, these hills were still populated by Comanche, and rightly so. This of course led to tension and the occasional unsolved murder on both sides. But perhaps more uncommon was Eanes's unmarked grave and the fact that, many years later, his skeleton was accidentally disturbed, hastily reburied, and left with only a thicket to remember him. Had this series of events roused his angry ghost?

It was during the 1960s that the larger gathering of Eanes-Marshall ghosts roused. This was a time when there were disputes within the family as to the ranch's ownership and, for this reason, it had fallen into near-ruin. In the early ghost-sightings, the ranch's early owner, Robert, appeared incoherently angry. His daughter, Viola, had been heard along the dark banks of Eanes Creek, crying for a lost love, killed—the story goes—by lightning; some old-time neighbors claimed to have seen her. Caretaker Cecil Johnson apparently heard laughter in the evenings that he recognized as the "cackle" of Hudson Marshall. Others witnesses, like neighbor Mike White, saw Hudson's upstairs porch rocker teetering away after dark. And down the ranch road there were sightings of that driverless ghost wagon.

The Bruce Marshalls were living in Houston when psychic teams determined to move in—naturally by night. Marshall accompanied the first group, principally San Antonians, together with Houston and Austin journalists and photographers. They used a method called "automatic writing" to make contact with the ghosts. One held the elbow of the other, who held the pencil. They first contacted Burns . . . or Barnes, the wagon driver, and discovered more of that story than ever before understood. The spirit described his ambush—three men, backshooting with rifles. When asked why he had been ambushed and shot, the spirit confessed:

he himself was a murderer. He had killed the woman he loved because she had rejected him. He had drowned her.

The spirit went on to explain that many spirits were in the vicinity. *Many are here,* the writing said, and almost immediately the Robert Eanes of long ago broke in. The writing became immediately violent; it was clear this spirit had something to tell. He was furious that no one would listen, and then the pencil broke.

At that point, the first medium became frightened, afraid to go on with it, and a second medium stepped in to try. This time, the paper tore and the pencil snapped again. And then something inexplicable happened.

The dead-still night became alive, and all at once a violent wind literally shook the old house. Then instant calm returned once more.

Could Robert have known who killed the wagon driver? Or was he furious with his daughter for loving that other man? Maybe he was angry over the ruin of his ranch?

After that, the psychics had to quit. They couldn't get through to Robert again.

It was a few years later, in 1969, that England's famed white witch Sybil Leek led another team of journalists to the ruin and its tangled land. She flatly refused any advance briefing as to the Eanes-Marshall story.

Seemingly unaware of those about her, Sybil withdrew into a corner of the night, and began to construct, via trance, much of what had happened so many years previous. She identified Robert Eanes as well as a man named Anderson, a man she described as having a lot to do with that place. And she identified a tree long ago scarred by lightning. She then envisioned an earlier homestead, a house built farther from the creek sitting under what is now Austin's Loop 360.

"Only my wife and I knew about that house," Bruce Marshall explained. "We had told nobody." Without a flashlight, Sybil Leek walked directly to the old cemetery where all of those bodies were buried, a spot you cannot find by day, unless guided. Finally she went straight to the lightning-struck tree, old and stark, where Viola's lover is said to have died in a flash.

"The only other time I heard Anderson's name mentioned," Bruce said, "was when my mother told me about him. Viola may have loved him, but she chose Hudson Marshall, who had money enough to hold the land. Anderson, it seems, wouldn't leave. And then he was struck by lightning."

Today the Eanes-Marshall Ranch seems quiet enough, though there remain many unanswered questions. Of course, as I told you at the beginning, this was to be no clear-cut story of ghosts, only a recounting of efforts to communicate with them. As I drove away that last day, a sudden rainstorm had overcome my camper van and me. Several close lightning bolts were followed by quick thunder, and I got on with my driving away.

THE CHISOS GUARDIAN

Chisos Mountains

For all the thirty miles southward from Persimmon Gap, the old war trail aims straight for the Big Bend's massive Chisos Mountains, looming ever larger like the ghosts their name suggests. As you climb from Tornillo Desert, they overpower the grasp of your visions. You are directly below their mightiest bastion, the towering Casa Grande.

Next time, study its west face closely. There, the profile is etched largely, and he is watching. Those who are wise in the mysteries of this lonely land know him. More, they know what he is watching for.

They could show you the cave where his mummy waited so long. On gloomy nights they have seen his watchfire. They know of secluded camps where sleepers waked to find moccasin tracks close around, close enough for sleeping faces to have been studied.

With wisdom given to the ancients, they even know why the sleepers were left unharmed.

Casa Grande's face belongs to Alsate, the last chieftain of the Chisos Apache. He stalks these nights. Searching for the descendants of the man who informed on his people. The man who brought the end to the Chisos Apache. Leoneceo Castillo.

Castillo was a double informer. To the Apache, forted in these crags, he warned of pursuing Mexican troops. Was he not of kindred Native blood?

Then to the Mexicans across the Chihuahua River, he foretold Apache raids. Was he not of kindred Mexican blood?

As thinning Apache ranks forced Alsate to cling only to the last mountain battlement of Casa Grande, the devious mind of Castillo saw one course—betray the losing side. What rewards would await the one who delivered every last Apache and Alsate himself!

Mexico listened.

From Chihuahua City in 1882, Castillo journeyed north into the stronghold of his Native kin. He bore a document bedecked with ribbon and gold seals—a full pardon for all if they came down off the peak.

The chief had heard of such pardons in America. The document was formidable, and his people, starving. After certain preliminary precautions Alsace's people came for a peace parley in San Carlos, Mexico.

There was a feast and rivers of mescal, then slumber. But when they awoke, they were manacled, and forced to march. Scattered across Mexico in servitude, the Apache were defeated.

Before he died in the struggles of his people attempting to flee, Alsate swore a great death oath against Castillo. Alive or dead he would track the man on earth and beyond.

Some disagree. There are tales that the chief, gravely wounded, managed his way back to the Casa Grande. Once there, he began his hunt for the betrayer of his people.

There are many tales of Alsate's return to the area. The chief was seen watching from high above Mariscal Canyon. In the night, flitting shadows were seen, moccasin prints left behind. Another claimed to know of a cave that the chief hid in during the day.

It was too much for Castillo. He abandoned his home and hid in the mountains that the Apache in him knew almost as well as the thing hunting him.

It is told by the old ones that Leoneceo suffered agonies known only to those whom death pursues. From cave shelter, he could look into black night—how could he dare a fire?—and know, as only Native eyes can, that he was watched.

When mountain wind rose with first dark, did he not hear more than wind? Did he not hear the blood oath of Alsate, whispered from the night?

Eventually Castillo fled far from these mountains, and almost immediately, the visitant was seen no more. The watch fires went out. There was no more talk of a waiting cave, or searching tracks.

Many said that finally, Alsate had died.

Hearing that the sightings had stopped, Castillo returned to his village. With the bravado that a successful spy must demonstrate if he is to regain acceptance by those of importance, he even ventured within Alsate's mountain fortress.

It is told that, very close, Castillo saw the cave. So close that he could not mistake what waited for him within it.

After that, very little has been spoken of the informer, for he disappeared entirely. Those who reject the spirit world and its phantasms are sure that the man finally and forever left the country.

But those steeped in the old ways—they know—say Castillo will never leave. Somewhere near the entrance of his cavern, Alsate has him.

Now many are prone to dismiss the story wholesale. Yet in the late 1800s hunters still found moccasin tracks close by in the morning ashes of their campfire. More recently, land surveyors have encountered them, too.

Some years ago, those who studied the Chisos caves for the relics of prehistoric man came upon something sufficient even to give scientists pause.

In one cave were the mummified remains of a Native man. Beside him, the smaller body of a woman. There were ashes from fires not so old, and a supply of ready wood.

Alsate? Why would he remain?

To hunt down, to the very last living soul, all of Leoneceo Castillo's family? We have been told that he already has done that. So you and I, my friend, can sleep without apprehension in Alsate's Chisos camps.

That is, unless he believes that we, too, might be what he hunts.

A turncoat, of course.

A GESTURE FROM BEYOND

San Elizario, Gonzales

There are those of us who believe we have heard from beyond the final door that death closes. A sound in the night, the apparition of lost loved ones, the feeling of not being alone. There are some who believe the door can be kept open.

There is the story of Ann Kubala's husband who promised to cause a picture to fall from its place on the wall. One year to the hour after his death, his portrait fell from the mantel, its supporting cord intact and its hook affixed in brick.

Harry Houdini tirelessly debunked ideas of an afterlife. Though even he vowed to attempt to speak from beyond. The plan was to send his wife a secret code from beyond the grave. Psychic Arthur Ford communicated that message three years after Houdini's death. Eventually this incident was proven to be a fake.

The question remains: are there ways that the door *can* be opened?

Historian Josephina Escajeda related the tale of Bartolo Mendoza, the first man to be hung in El Paso County.

August 1868 was a grim month for the small town of San Elizario. An unbreakable drought ravaged farms in the area. The crops were only a few days away from a complete loss. To add to their troubles, Bartolo Mendoza had murdered his stepdaughter.

At his trial he showed only a deep and profound remorse, but attempted no defense. From his small prison cell he watched as they built the scaffold. On his knees, rosary in hand, Bartolo prayed relentlessly. As each day dragged his hanging nearer, his only emotion seemed to be a desperate effort to ready himself for an accounting to his Maker.

Rumors of his piety spread. The townsfolk claimed that he was not praying for forgiveness, that he knew better. There was speculation that he was praying for relief from the fear rising in him, for a quick end, for rest for his daughter's soul. As the rumors spread, Bartolo continued to pray.

The night before the execution was dry and hot as a furnace. The wind from the mountains was hot enough to ignite the brittle crops where they stood. At the appointed time, the guard entered the cell and asked Bartolo to rise. The condemned man was hollow-looking and tired.

"Bartolo." The guard didn't know what prompted him to speak, but he did. "You will soon come face-to-face with God. Before we are all ruined, can you ask Him to send a little rain?"

Bartolo's face calmed. The guard would later say that he seemed at peace.

The next afternoon, the guard escorted the prisoner out to the scaffold, and the execution was performed as scheduled. At three o'clock Bartolo Mendoza was hung.

Above the gallows, the sky was cloudless and blue. Signs of heat rose from the ground. They took Bartolo down from the scaffold and started toward the cemetery.

As they walked the short distance, the sky suddenly boiled and grew black. The rain was heavy and continuous. For exactly twenty-four hours it fell. Then the people of San Elizario knew what Bartolo had been praying for. For Bartolo, his final minutes were spent searching for one final good act he might be able to do.

The other tale is the story of Gonzales County's fifth and final hanging on March 18, 1921, as told to me by Nancy Voigt of the Gonzales Chamber of Commerce.

The Gonzales County Jail is a forbidding three-story brick building that was completed in 1887. The site welcomes three thousand visitors a year. They wander through its dungeon like rooms and marvel at the two-story cages in the main prison area. Most impressive, though, is the gallows.

Directly outside and facing the cages, the two-story contraption stands like a grisly throne. To those awaiting the death sentence it embodied the constant promise of death. Even today, it is the image visitors will carry away with them.

Throughout his trial, Albert Howard insisted he was innocent of the charges leveled against him. This despite his prior convictions and even one jailbreak on his record. After his conviction and sentencing, he swore that they were about to hang an innocent man. He continued to swear this until his death.

Albert took his place in the cells of Gonzales County in January 1921 to wait out the two months before execution. Out his window the gallows stood awaiting him. For Albert Howard, though, there was something else out those windows that would prove to be more troublesome.

The current Gonzales County Courthouse was finished in 1896. The three-story building is in the Second Empire style. There are columns of every size and style, dormers, arches, cupolas, turrets, and balconies. Of all its features, the three-story clock tower dominates.

From his cell, Albert could see the north face of this clock tower. It was in that building that he faced trial and sentencing. It was into this clock face that Albert would channel his anger. How many days were left? How many hours? Minutes? Seconds?

Far worse than the gallows right outside his window was watching the final few hours, minutes, and seconds of his life slide away; it became an obsession. He began to talk to anyone who would listen about the damnable clock and how he wished something would stop its steady march.

He vowed that the clock would mark his death and then never again count time against any man. Eventually the guards and other prisoners all knew of his oath.

March 18 came.

The clock could not announce the date, but it could name the hour; Albert Howard was hung on schedule at seven-fifteen.

The clock on the courthouse never again kept the right time, each face on its own schedule. In the 1980s and again in the 1990s the clock was completely renovated with great cost to donors and city officials.

As I left the Chamber of Commerce after speaking to Nancy Voigt I couldn't help but stare up at the clock. It was precisely five o'clock. I circled the baroque old courthouse. Not one face agreed.

MISTER DIENGER

Boerne

When we think of ghosts, we think of tortured souls left to wander the earth. These are stories to raise the hairs on the back of your neck. In this light, it seems disrespectful to call Joseph Dienger a ghost. He is certainly not malevolent, though he does bump in the night.

Over the last century the Dienger building has been a grocery store, a boarding house, a meeting place, a feed store, a private club, a restaurant and bar, a library, and a cultural center. The home was listed as a Texas Historic Landmark in 1982 and then added to the National Register of Historic Places in 1984. Initially built by Joseph Dienger in the 1880s to house his country store, the ground floor was a large open space full of shelves and bins atop a stone-walled cellar where meats were hung and wines cooled. The second story was added to house Joseph, his wife Ida, and their seven children. On that floor was also a large community room for the town's general use.

Antlers, a restaurant and lounge, occupied the large room on the second floor of the Dienger building during the 1970s. Within the restaurant, the Trophy Room had been the Diengers' bedroom, where in 1950, at the age of 90, Joseph died.

Over its life the restaurant had several owners. One of them, Doris Rankin, sat down with me to tell of her time at the Dienger building.

It was late in the evening, and Doris and her teenage daughter, Lorena, were closing the bar when loud footsteps sounded on the covered stairs that were the only entrance in and out of the establishment. Doris's husband, Rex, came into the room looking confused. "Very late for a customer."

Without fanfare or acknowledgment a short, compact man in a dark suit walked in. He had on old-fashioned square spectacles and was in a hurry to cross the space. He walked past the bar and the three Rankins, disappearing into a small room adjacent to the bar: the Trophy Room.

The Rankins looked at each other in shock. It was unusual to have a customer this late; their patrons knew and respected their hours. Rex shrugged. Lorena walked over to the door and peered inside the small, dark room.

She turned quickly. "There's nobody there!"

The room's only other exit opened onto the covered gallery that wrapped around the second floor of the building. The family searched the gallery and the yard below, but it was obvious the man had not jumped.

One theory is that the man was Joseph Dienger, who, along with his wife, was known to dislike drinking. The Rankins were well-acquainted with this aspect of the original owners. From the opening of Antlers, they believe Dienger continued to demonstrate—in gentlemanly, if persistent fashion—his disapproval. Doors slammed and windows rattled. Lights flickered in the dark cellar. "Mister Dienger," Rex Rankin would comment, "is making lots of racket tonight."

Ida let her presence be known in a more discreet manner. Once, Doris looked up from a lounge table to see, crossing toward the Trophy Room, the silhouette of a woman in a bodice and flowing skirts, her long hair pulled up in a severe bun. The shadow passed through the solid wall into what was once the Dienger bedroom.

"We found out later that the bedroom door had been right there." She pointed to the place the figure walked through. Today that spot is a solid wall.

Others who have operated Antlers suspected themselves guests of the Diengers. One spring night, Mrs. Adrien White glanced up to see a woman with long hair, clad in an eyelet slip and camisole, walk directly through a closed door. And Bob Pegram, who in 1968 first converted the building to a restaurant-lounge, exhibited such awed courtesy toward its longtime owners that he maintained a complete table setting at the door to the Trophy Room.

Down through the years, that custom did not change. Over the table, always an immaculate spread, Dienger's handsome red lamp above, and in the thin-stemmed crystal goblet, the drink he favored—cool, straight up, water.

"No one was allowed to touch that table," Judy Watson told me. She owned the restaurant just before the Rankins. "If they left papers or things on it, we'd find them on the floor. Sometimes the glass would be half-empty."

She admitted that she never actually saw either of the Diengers, but she heard them. "He banged on doors, locked them, rattled the windows, turned lights on and off. Once we had a party, and Jerry Bailey— he's the automobile dealer and, believe me, the very last man to accept the idea of ghosts—came out of the bathroom in a hurry. Someone had tapped him on the shoulder; when he turned, Mister Dienger stood there, just staring at him."

There is another story of the spirit pulling a chair out from a table for a woman with her hands full.

"When we were real busy, he was very courteous about helping . . . but not where drinks were being served." Judy Watson smiled as she related this.

Judy decided to open the restaurant on Sundays, and explained that Joseph was against this. He would lock the door as soon as she unlocked it. "Oh, I'd get put out," she recalled. "I'd say, 'Mister Dienger, you *know* that I have a business to run. Now you leave this door alone!'"

She spoke to him daily. "I'd open up and say, 'Good morning, Mister Dienger,' and late each night as I turned off the lights, I'd call out, 'See you in the morning.'"

She was unafraid. "I suppose he was annoying at times. I'd be working downstairs, and he'd start banging things up in the lounge. I'd call to him that he wasn't behaving as a gentleman would, and the banging would stop. I'd say he was a friend."

With each new tenant, Mister Dienger introduces himself. At the end of the seventies the restaurant closed and First National Bank moved in. Garland Perry was the director of business development. "Occasionally, when I know I've turned off the cellar lights the night before, I'll find them on in the morning. Of course, we don't serve drinks." Perry laughed and recalled a party they held in the large upstairs room. In several of the pictures a strange opaque figure appears alongside the guests, "If the tenants are nice—if he likes them—he'll let them stay."

What else would you expect from a well-respected southern gentleman?

EDITOR'S NOTE: In 1989, the Dienger Building was purchased by the City of Boerne. After a significant remodel, it was reopened in 1991 as the new home to the Boerne Public Library.

THE SEARCHER

Laredo, Rancho Dolores

Ahead in the darkness the small light moved. It swung, like a lantern held in the hands of someone unsure of the rocky terrain. The young man took a step forward and it drew away, taunting him to follow . . . into the night, away from the little lamps of his village.

With certainty, the young man knew it for a ghost light.

From where he stood, just up the shoulder of the tailings from the mine, he could see where the horizon flattened out as it neared Laredo. The tailings made a dark hillock beside the dimness of his village. All about was a black night, even across the border in Mexico.

Slowly the light went into the chaparral-covered rocky expanse toward the far hill that marked the abandoned mine. Which spirit was this? The young man regretted that his mescal was finished. His feet were unsteady on the rocks, but still he followed. The beckoning light bobbing ahead cast human-like shadows in every direction. Which spirit was it? He knew of two tales.

Rancho Dolores ran graded Herefords on several thousand acres alongside the Rio Grande, twenty-five miles west of Laredo. Ted Scibienski occupied singular ground—his ranch was the site of a ghost town sitting above a ghost mine on land where a ghostly lantern stalks the night.

His ranch also sat over a bonanza of bright-burning, if smoky, cannel coal. Its presence is what brought about the two specters.

In 1880, when coal was king, former Colorado governor Alexander Cameron Hunt opened the first large-scale mine in the area. Its tunnels formed a two-layer labyrinth. The hundred-foot-deep shafts reached two miles back from the river bluff. The governor's town, a sprawl of thatch and adobe, was called Minera, population five thousand.

As veins played out, Minera moved with the new works, leaving her ruins behind in the brush. The 1920s brought oil production and soon all that remained were the ruins. Traces remain—concrete foundations and collapsed airshafts. The big, stained hills, and tailing piles from those dark, hidden tunnels below. Today the population is only twenty.

The last mine commissary is now a storage barn for the ranch, which remembers those early days with its name—Dolores.

Dolores was also the name of an eighteen-year-old servant girl in Governor Hunt's home. She was a miner's daughter who was said to be one of the most beautiful girls in the area.

To the Hunt home came a handsome young Pennsylvanian, a graduate engineer. The improbable, but perhaps inevitable, happened—the engineer and Dolores fell in love. What at first seemed inconsequential to Governor Hunt was now a problem: these two intended to marry. To avoid disgrace, the young engineer was sent home.

In broken Spanish, he told Dolores he would come back. In broken English, she told him she would wait. He wrote, but because she could not read, nor trust another to write him what remained in her heart, she never responded. The letters lessened, then ceased.

Dolores sickened with grief, but she had sworn to wait, and she knew he must return. Crying hopelessly, she wandered the bare hills they had walked together. Eventually, as the old ones knew they must, they found her at the bottom of a hundred-foot airshaft.

Yet, as these old ones knew they would, they saw her return. After twilight, she was out there in the black, windy dark, walking the hills with her lantern, waiting.

But is it always the lantern of the distraught girl? The mescal in the young man's veins made him sad for Dolores. A kind man would follow and attempt to comfort such a sorrowful ghost. The mescal also made him forget the danger that was said to be out in the hills. For there was another who stalked the night.

The searcher.

The warnings said that you shouldn't follow this ghost. But a brave man might take the chance . . . and be rewarded.

Some tell of a bandito leader who accumulated great stolen wealth. What better place to hide it than in these deserted, pitch-black shafts? Every person up to no good used those shafts to hide treasure. As the mines were abandoned, the better the hiding.

The bandito was a cruel and frightened man; a gang leader must always fear his second in command—why should that man not wish to be first? To avoid this, the leader would periodically kill his lieutenants—a solution practical to him and one that continued until his uneasy band turned on him violently.

While secreting new treasure in the darkest reach of the mines, they fell upon their leader with pickaxes and knives, and then walled off what remained of him. Time passed and the crew returned to collect the treasure. The story goes that they found the wall they had built broken down, the body of their former leader missing.

Had he not died? Perhaps his soul had breached the tomb walls, vengeful, using the searching light to lure victims to the same fate that befell him. What a fearful last mortal sight—to confront that dead lamp-lit face.

Over confidential tequilas in remote cantinas across that brasada, it was whispered that after the man's death the hills became unsafe for secreting treasure or retrieving what had been hidden. Those who attempted, it was said, died horribly in the night, or were found wandering the hills, insane, terror frozen on their faces.

And so, behind the light that wanders about these lonely, darkened hillocks, you can see that there is dangerous uncertainty. Which fate awaits you? One would hope, as did that brave young man who opened this story, to look on the beauty of Dolores.

It is told, however, that the young man was found in first light—broken, deranged, and babbling incoherently.

Some believe that he is now in the old graveyard at Rancho Dolores, where the plastic flowers stand fresh by the crosses, and where some of the old ones, the ones from the time of the mines, still come back on Sundays. You can visit here; perhaps they will tell you more.

Rancho Dolores, of course, is private. This is all for the best. You could so easily follow the wrong lantern.

EDITOR'S NOTE: The original form of this story appeared in the December 8, 1963, edition of the *Victoria Advocate*.

There were a few liberties taken in the telling of this story, or maybe the locals took a few liberties in telling it to Ed. It is possible that Rancho Dolores took its name from the young girl who haunts the former mine, but the sprawling ranch is more likely named for the neighboring town of Dolores.

That town was established as a Mexican village named San José in 1860. The Cannel Coal Company opened the first mines in the 1880s and built the Rio Grande and Eagle Pass Railroad to ship coal from them. The president of that company, David Darwin Davis, had a daughter named Dolores. The town's name was changed in her honor. Even though there is no record of Dolores Davis dying tragically, it is possible that the "miner's daughter" was actually the CEO's.

The population Ed gives for Minera (5,000) is very high for a small mining town of the time period. The highest recorded population found today comes from the 1900 census—1,022 men, women, and children. The town began to decline immediately after this due to oil production and the location of the mine itself.

It is possible that Ed is citing the population for the entire area from the late 1800s. Historically four mining towns existed; their highest recorded populations added together still only account for around 3,822 people—Santo Tomás (1,000), Minera (1,022), Darwin (800), and Dolores (1,000). It is possible that the number includes the population for Laredo, which in the 1880s was around 3,500. All of the now-ghost towns sit within Laredo's jurisdiction today, and are located in a small geographic region, so the combination is not unreasonable.

PHANTOM ON THE MOUNTAIN

Fredericksburg

My grandson Richard knew the tales of an accursed Native chief who roamed the mesa above our campsite. We had pitched our camp in a little oak grove beside the creek, having finished discovering arrowheads and scrapers and knives of those long-ago people. In the morning we would climb to the top; now, our campfire was dozing in its bed of orange embers.

"Does he really have to stay up there, Granddaddy?"

"He can't come down here," I assured. "The curse won't let him."

Richard seemed unconvinced, but we settled down for sleep.

It was late when he waked me suddenly.

"He's up there, Granddaddy. I can see him!"

Behind the enormous mass, looming blacker than the night all about, heat lightning flickered away to the west; it etched that high rim against the sky.

There was a big shadow near the top. It had to be the immense granite block that looks like a speck by day. And that muttering sound from beyond our dead fire? It must be the wind. Those flickering lights near the summit? There was no moon . . . a reflection from lightning?

"I don't see anything," I said.

"I saw him," Richard insisted, then fell into a silence which considered creatures that were terrible enough to sacrifice boys and girls.

"I promise you, he can't come down here," I repeated. But the words felt meaningless.

Long before that night the Tonkawa, Apache, and Comanche people dwelt in the land now called Texas. This land was hard: its beasts were ferocious, food was only what could be gathered or killed, and enemies were all about. At times human sacrifice was practiced to appease the gods, though accounts vary on this.

One such god lived deep within an immense rock, and to the people below this was a temple mound. It was the more marvelous because there it stood mightily, placed by the spirits themselves, and far bigger than those pyramid-shaped temples the other tribes—those far to the south—had built of rock, or even those made of dirt, as wanderers found to the east.

Such a god would be satisfied with sacrifice of only the fairest of the young: the boy or girl led to the summit, where stone knives cut out hearts and prayerful hands splashed blood, great altar fires consuming what was left.

One chieftain had sickened of the sacrifices—good times had not been restored. Dire times were leading toward dire actions. The chief came to the conclusion that only the blood of his daughter would satisfy the thirst of the rock.

The spirit, who had no interest in sacrifices, was incensed by this transgression: a fearful roar rose up, the very rock itself shook, while the sacrificial fire blew across the mountaintop to flicker in a hundred tiny tongues. The chieftain vanished.

But he was not entirely dead, his people were told. Rather, he was drawn within the great rock and was there imprisoned whenever the light of day touched the temple mound. When night came, he was released, and back and forth across the lofty summit he was condemned to walk in penance. He must walk that way forever—his curse!

From father to son, as these ancients knew their history, the story was passed along. All people knew its meaning: never again could a

Native man set foot upon that height; let the sacrifices be offered only in the huge boulders at its foot.

The boulders are still there, rust-red and house-sized, scattered as by a giant hand around the base of an enormous granite dome that dominates our Hill Country of today. This is Enchanted Rock, north of Fredericksburg, halfway to Llano.

The Comanche both feared and revered the gigantic red dome, a fact known to one of Texas's most intrepid rangers, Captain Jack Hays. In 1841, when these hills were a wide-walled and deadly Comanche fortress, Hays rode up to survey new country and, on a crisp autumn morning, found himself near the looming mass.

Near too, were Native horsemen who had cut his trail to the tiny settlement of Fredericksburg. Hays dropped his Jacob's staff, vaulted into his saddle, and raced for the rock. Straight up it he rode, finally scrambling afoot to its naked summit where, with two Navy Colt five-shooters and his rifle, he could look down on a hundred warriors circling the three-mile base below.

History—there is a bronze plaque near the top—tells that the ranger held that summit, but Hays, wise in the ways of the Natives, understood what had saved his life. The Comanche knew that no Native man climbed the rock and lived.

Had the ranger remained up there through the night, he might have come down a different man. He might have seen the death fires that dance the rims; he might have heard the devil-voices below in the rock. He might even have seen the ghost warriors walk the eternal dark.

We, of course, are sure only of what science tells us. A granite mass, chilling from the day's heat, will shift with deep whispers. The slit caves atop and up the sheer west wall are simply split-off faults. The tomb-hollow feel under your feet—there seems almost an echo—results from loosening granite layers below you.

And the Native ghost lights? The mica in granite can reflect moonlight, and so can the tiny rain pools that fleck the slopes and stand wind-rippled atop. There is nothing more up there, says science, than old, old legend. That, of course, and a magnificent view that you can reach with a surprisingly easy climb along a marked trail.

From the broad, flat top you can see Bullhead Mountain and Smoothing Iron, rearing above lesser rims to the northwest; to the east, the Riley Mountains make a long blue wall. Just below are craggy Turkey Peak and a phalanx of smaller domes. Yours is the height of a fifty-story building, a pinkish-red canopy of granite second in size only to Georgia's Granite Mountain, and broad enough at the base to cover a seven hundred-acre farm.

Around the circular foot are the sheared-off house-sized boulder formations like the Queen's Chair and the Council of Witches; it is not too hard to envision human sacrifices in those strange red temples, and they take you back to a time before that of the Druids.

Such a time, of course, leaves you confronted with that ancient Native chieftain who nightly walks the dark summit. You are reminded of him by the little potholes at the very top. For countless centuries, water— quite naturally—has worked them into the eternal granite.

It is only coincidence that they string across the heights, a stride apart, and that they form precise moccasin prints.

Although they are aware of him in the state park below, rangers smile when considering Enchanted Rock's phantom. Among the observers I know personally, only my grandson Richard has seen the ghost.

I suspect that any seven-year-old boy who camps with you along Sandy Creek, near the base, will confirm his sighting.

Our night passed uneventful after Richard's sighting, though neither of us slept. I watched the sun rise through the trees. After coffee, then breakfast, we climbed to the top of the rock.

"You see." I pointed to the huge granite block near the top. "That's what you were looking at."

"It was over here." Richard scooted across the top and was looking at the procession of potholes. "Does water really make these?"

"Yes," I said. "It takes a long time."

"Granddaddy, why do they look like footprints?"
I smiled. For the life of me, I didn't have an answer.

EDITOR'S NOTE: The American version of the Jacob's staff was an early surveying instrument—predating the tripod—that consisted of a single pole on which to secure a compass.

LA LLORONA

Waco

When, on a wintry morning, Shirley Mackie ventured outside her home near Lake Waco, she sought only to photograph the misty beauty of the snowscape. She never suspected that she was about to revive one of this land's oldest legends.

Later I was in the Mackie home, whose handsome grounds back onto cliff-girt Hog Creek above the lake, and Shirley showed me an enlargement of the picture she took. What did I see?

Ice-palace beauty certainly, the great tall trees all diamond-dusted, and far below its rocky cliff, the broad creek frozen to silver. But high on a promontory not fifty feet from the camera's eye, I distinguished the hazy outlines of something else.

"A woman, and the baby she's holding," I said.

"To the naked eye," Shirley Mackie retorted, "she wasn't there at all."

I thought of the many who, for centuries, have told of seeing others like her. Near dark riverbanks from El Paso to Laredo, and Victoria to San Marcos, such penitent vigil has been observed, stubbornly reported and equally ridiculed.

This is La Llorona, the spectral woman weeping for her crime. Throughout Central and South American communities, stories persist of the spectral figure of the woman who drowned her newborn and has been condemned to return without rest.

Skeptics see no more than fanciful legend passed along in a hundred variants, from South America to Mexico to California. Represented in the post-colonization myths of many Hispanic cultures, the story of the weeping woman searching for her lost children shows up in ancient Aztec, Greek, and Slavic folktales as well. The lost child, a powerful image.

But is this pure fiction?

Not to this photograph, the one sitting before me that seemed to have captured her.

Shirley Mackie looked much younger than her fiftyish years, and her forthright manner concealed the sensitivity of a musician. She was this state's first female band director, and as she found beauty in music, she also saw it framed in nature: photography had long been her hobby. And so on that snowy morning in 1978, she saw the picture she had to take.

She took me outside. We walked toward the cliff, jagged in outthrust rock seventy feet above water. "I stood here," she said, looking over the edge.

"I shot downstream to get the whole setting." Then she pointed at an overhang not far away. "That's where the camera found her."

Her Minolta revealed a young woman with long hair, a cape, and a baby, blanket-wrapped and cradled in her arms. Now the sycamore and elm below were in full, warm leaf, and the normally wide creek, low in dry summer. I thought of the biting cold that drove Shirley indoors, and then of the woman who must have remained to suffer through it.

"I put the camera away," Shirley said. "I didn't finish the roll until May. It was only when I studied the prints that I discovered what I had shot."

She knew little of the legend La Llorona, and nothing of a woman in the area of her home. Yet, what was it, standing on that frigid edge of rock?

For a time she showed her photograph only to friends. What did they see?

"The same thing you did," she told me. "They thought they saw a ghost."

By August, Shirley's curiosity had firmed to resolve: by sharing the picture, something might be learned. Carol Daniel of Waco's *Tribune Herald* wrote the story, and carried a sketch of the photograph: its hazy color made reproduction difficult. In some respects, the larger story began at that time.

A neighbor, long in residence nearby, called to say that since she'd been a child, she had known of this woman: a legend handed down, from how long ago, nobody knew—perhaps from earliest days when all this was open range. There had been a girl, a pretty one . . . one with an illegitimate child. In shame, she threw the infant from this cliff. Later, tormented by grief and horror, she died.

That she could not leave that easily was known to ranch hands of the latter 1800s. On the cliff, by day or night, they saw her. Who she was, they could not or would not tell. That was all the neighbor knew; it was long ago.

Lorenzo Gayton was one. He came to Shirley's home with a copy of the newspaper. Nearing fifty and living in Waco, he had grown up on the ranch across Hog Creek. It was a time when all about was a fine emptiness, where a boy could hunt squirrel or rabbit, or fish in the deep creek. Might he see the photograph?

"Mr. Gayton studied it a long time," Shirley recalled, and then he told her, "Miss Mackie, I want you to know I am completely sober, and I am also a good Christian." He was looking her straight in the eye, and went on to say it was the same woman he'd seen as a boy.

He had been hunting along the lower, opposite bank. And right there he had seen movement and he'd swung up his rifle. Squarely in his sights, a woman stood poised on this rocky point, a woman with a baby held just that way, dressed just that way. He had gestured toward the photograph. While he stared, she had disappeared, he explained. It had so frightened him that he told only his parents; his brother and friends surely would laugh at him.

Lorenzo later learned that his brother would not have laughed. That he too, had seen La Llorona, and more than once. The last time was when the older brother came home to forget World War II. Walking along the creekside tranquility was his way of forgetting, and he preferred to go alone.

From one such walk, the brother returned to his house, badly shaken. "She's still there," he told Lorenzo, and then for two weeks, as though in shock, he spoke very little at all.

Before coming to the Mackie residence, Lorenzo had stopped at a home across the creek, a friend whose family had lived on this land longer than anyone, a man whose reticence often concealed what he knew. Yes, the old man told Lorenzo, he was aware of the woman on the cliff.

The man, and his family before him, had seen her many times. They kept the matter to themselves, certainly the fact that more than once they had heard the infant's cry as it fell. People wouldn't understand.

"A lot of people seemed to understand." Shirley Mackie looked at her photograph. "You'd be amazed how many people I've heard from . . . and all over."

Yet none of them knew—or cared to tell—the identity of this lady on the cliff. Nor, despite research, could reporter Carol Daniel disclose it. Perhaps Native? Perhaps pioneer—Mexican or Anglo?

"You do know the story of La Llorona?" I asked Lorenzo Gayton later.

"Yes," he said. "But I didn't know that she could be photographed."

You will understand why Shirley Mackie asks that I obscure her address; the curious would swarm her grounds, and the cliff could be dangerous.

No, she didn't mind me sharing her name, nor her belief that her camera indeed had discerned something from the spirit world, something invisible to mortal eyesight. It had happened once before in a vacant cathedral in France when, very young, she studied music in Europe. The film revealed hazy figures kneeling beside the empty altar.

How could the camera achieve what the eye could not? Some believe that the heat generated by a spirit's presence can imprint itself on film; she's been told that. Did I have another theory?

I had none beyond a decreasing skepticism as to old legend. Perhaps the old and wise even today see La Llorona along the Rio Grande near the ruins of ancient Presidio San Vicente. Perhaps they hear the infant's cry, dropped from the cliffs below Mariscal Canyon. Perhaps San Antonio indeed has a Donkey Lady. Perhaps we aren't to know such things.

Perhaps, as Shirley Mackie contends, it is a mistake for any of us to say, "This—or that—cannot be."

"Who," she asks, "wants to walk through all the wonders of this life with a mind that closed?"

EDITOR'S NOTE: The legend of La Llorona has hundreds of variations all over the areas of North and South America that were colonized by Spain. The most common is of a woman who drowns her children to get revenge on a cheating husband. She is then refused entry into the afterlife until she can locate her dead children. She wanders, looking for them. In some variations, she steals the children of others in an attempt to drown them. In all versions she is considered a bad omen if seen.

The closest record outside of Ed's retelling of the Lake Waco ghost is from 160 miles to the southwest. Hollering Woman Creek is between San Antonio and Seguin; stories of mysterious screaming and hazy female figures on the banks of this seasonal creek have been told across the centuries.

THE LADY IN GREEN

San Patricio, Nueces

In the early 1830s, upriver from Corpus and a few miles south of Mathis, stood the log walls of Mexico's Fort Lipantitlan. Today, the Nueces bottoms are tangled in hackberry, mesquite, and huisache—the fort is virtually traceless. In those trouble times, though, the fort was an important barrier against further Anglo colonization

This was with good cause. In 1829 James McGloin and John McMullen were granted special approval from the Mexican government to bring two hundred Irish settlers to form the outpost of San Patricio. There were initial tensions between the new settlement and its fortified neighbor, but Lipantitlan's commandant, the handsome and urbane young Marcelino Garcia, became a good friend of the Irish settlers, and many of the problems quieted.

In the home of James McGloin, empresario of that steadily thriving and southwesternmost Texas colony, the young captain was often a welcome guest. Frequently, the two spoke of Marcelino's sweetheart, faraway in Mexico City. Soon she would be his bride and join him. Although frontier life would be hard, and she would be one of the few women at the fort, Marcelino hoped the women of San Patricio would soften her isolation.

If only the damnable troubles between Mexico and Texas could be settled amicably! Of that darkening shadow, the two friends spoke more and more guardedly; and the young captain found his own expressions necessarily becoming those of a soldier of his country. The wedge between the friends grew over time.

San Patricio had few defenses outside a single cannon. Santa Anna's orders to Lipantitlan were explicit: take the cannon. It fell on Marcelino to figure out how to do this without offending his friend. In desperation, the young captain "borrowed" the fieldpiece. But to the north now, there was shooting at Gonzales and even San Antonio. The Irish would need their gun returned. Marcelino saw no choice but to face his friend with the truth: his orders forbade its return.

At the time there were only two Mexican forts in the area, Lipantitlan and the Alamo. The majority of the troops from Lipantitlan were spread thinly and the fort was rarely fully protected.

From the east, more Texans arrived; and in the Texan capture of Lipantitlan, Marcelino Garcia was gravely wounded. Following the capture in November 1835, the fort was completely dismantled.

Into his home across the river, McGloin carried his friend: somehow he might be saved, and more importantly, he must get word to the girl in Mexico. By whatever means, he managed the letter and its courier.

The winter days turned bleaker, then the dripping skies and the young commandant's condition worsened. But the captain clung to life, waiting for word from his love. The priest prepared for last rites. It was then that the visitant appeared.

Several were in the room when she came through the unopened door. First glimpse revealed only great beauty under her mantilla, a green silk gown with black polka dots, the grace and carriage of a lady of quality.

She moved without sound, without a glance to either side, directly to Marcelino's bed. The dying man saw her; he reached up as though having known all that time that she must come. His circling arms passed through the seeming substance of the woman's body.

Silence gripped the others while she stood beside the bed, a delicate hand seeming to rest on his brow. How long—who was sure? Did she disappear? Or did she leave as she had come: through a closed door? Had she been there at all?

Indeed she had: she returned the following day . . . and the next. She was there when the young officer released his life. She did not follow to the cemetery on the little hill; she appeared to know only where his friend had carried her husband-to-be.

She had come so often that those of the McGloin household felt no fear of her, and no longer, any surprise. To them, she had come to be simply the "woman in green." Perhaps a sort of Irish acceptance of the strangeness in the world.

Yet surprise awaited them in the end. Young Marcelino was cold in his grave, yet the visitant continued to return. By the empty bed she stood briefly, looking down as though he were still there.

How, in Mexico City, could she know that her lover had died? She would have known of the wound, of where he lay suffering—the courier with that letter. McGloin wondered if he should write again? How could he, with war at the doorstep?

Of what happened during the next few months when San Patricio was taken by Santa Anna's forces, no one can be certain. Then the war was over.

Returning to his home, a thunderstruck James McGloin found the woman yet constant, returning each day for bedside vigil. Always she came in the same silent unawareness of any other presence, always lovely in the same green gown, the same mantilla. Always and completely unchanged in the beauty of youth. For twenty-five years McGloin descendants witnessed those visitations. Then they stopped. I suppose one could argue that James McGloin had built himself a new house, away from the old Constitution Square and by Round Lake, the bedside she had known no longer present for her vigil.

But a more likely explanation is that her visits ended almost precisely when she died—a fact the McGloins were later to learn. The family accepted this: the two had again joined and were now one, together in a dimension closed even to Gaelic understanding.

And so it was that I took directions at the Old San Patricio Store, and drove back roads leading around to the onetime crossing below the granite marker noting Fort Lipantitlan's site.

A Texas Historic Park, it is small and lonely, with mesquite shade above a few picnic tables, the interlacing snarl of timber and brush immediately beyond a string of fence, toward the river.

I suppose you could manage a camp here, though facilities don't provide for it. However, I was wondering how long one must stay before glimpsing the two of them. It would not be to San Patricio they would come: Lipantitlan was to be their first home.

I'm sure that some of you will agree that these two must return—such devotion guarantees it—and that here is where they would come. Perhaps I should have waited. Others of you, I suspect, will dismiss the whole matter to my Irish vagaries.

My good friend Bill Walraven wrote about the Lady in Green for the *Corpus Christi Caller Times*. Once, deep in conversation, we were considering her when conversation turned to the Russians. Bear with me; this relates to our story. We discussed the possibility that the Russians were deep into the research of thought projection. Doubtless, so were we. Think yourself to Mars, for example, and in that instant, you are there. In the vague focus of such a premise, Bill holds that the tale of this lady is not *just* a story about a mysterious visitant.

EDITOR's NOTE: Bill Walraven died in 2013, at the age of 88. He wrote several books on Texas history that are still in print.

There is a variant of this story that says the woman in green was a young Irish girl that James McGloin knew before leaving Ireland. She swore she would haunt him for leaving her behind. While that is not a threat to be taken lightly, Ed's story seems closer to known historic events.

James McGloin died in 1856. Both his and Marcelino Garcia's graves were marked by wooden crosses and are lost to history.

BEND OF THE RIVER

San Marcos River

The San Marcos River wanders crystalline through great stands of pecan and cypress—old country, first a Spanish settlement, later a white sea of cotton plantations, and now drowsy with little strung-along downstream villages, Martindale, Fentress, and Prairie Lea.

By day, the bottoms are park-like in beauty. By night, when the times of year are right, these woodlands can become a misty mid-region where some believe several phantoms wander.

Now, San Marcos is home to many ghostly stories. Several of them date from the Civil War. One such tale recounts a squad of Confederate soldiers dispatched to Thompson's Island to investigate continuous terrifying screams. When they arrived they discovered a small cabin engulfed in flames, the occupants of the house all dead inside. A strange woman stood off to the side smiling oddly in the dark. She was badly burned over most of her body, and as the men approached, she vanished into the mists of dawn.

While this story is gruesome, there are other less disturbing tales along the river.

Mrs. Frances Stoval drove me along the backroads that explore this wooded riverside. A leader in San Marcos's exceptional historic renovations, she was admittedly more interested in the history of the ancient crossing, but the old tales of specters also intrigued her; she would not entirely rule them out. Heritage is heritage, she said, and she knew the stories of the woman who walks the night at Thompson's Island.

The islet, southeast of the city where the Blanco and San Marcos rivers converge, was originally part of the William Alexander Thompson Plantation, and across that rich land in early days ran a swift millrace.

Postwar reconstruction beset the plantation with hard times: the struggle to change a way of life, to survive the vise of Federal occupation, to house slaves who had been "freed" into homelessness, to rise above despair.

One who could not rise was a pretty young woman—it is not clear whether she was single or war-widowed—who found herself carrying an illegitimate child. She bore the child, but shame mounted to desperation: on a black night, she threw her baby into the millrace. On the instant of the act, she broke—near mad with horror—at what she had done.

Night after night, in awful penance, she walked the riverbank gloom, keening uncontrollably. Those who saw and heard knew that nothing could be done for her.

"Along the river at that time," Frances Stovall explained, "the Thompsons had helped their former slaves build their shacks." She gestured downstream where the San Marcos makes a sweeping bend and disappears in the shadow of big pecans.

"Naturally, they saw her each night," she said. "They heard her and . . . well, it would be frightening to anyone."

"And then she died." I jumped ahead.

Mrs. Stovall nodded. "And they continued to see and hear her. Some, they say, believe they still do. When the mist rises down here, it gets pretty eerie."

I had already talked with Mrs. Kathryn Rich, a descendant of the Thompsons, and she was not so sure of the story. At night, she confided, some of the Thompson boys were said to have gone down to the river with sheets over their heads. Perhaps the ghost was no more than that.

I have learned never to debate believers or disbelievers, for both are generally resolute. And so I began thinking of a former classmate of mine, Dr. Roy A. Pennycuick, a San Antonio professor. Not far from Thompson's Island, Roy encountered this river's other phantom, and his experience is not so easily shrugged off.

In 1939, just out of school, Roy worked for the General Motors Acceptance Corporation. Late one Saturday night in autumn, he was returning from South Texas with a coworker. They had some $25,000 in collected GMAC funds and wanted it locked in a safe as soon as possible. Over a weekend, a police station safe offered the best protection. To speed the delivery, they took a backroad shortcut, though both were apprehensive about this. A few dark miles short of San Marcos, right as they were crossing the old river bridge, a tire blew out, and they stopped to hurriedly change it.

While working quickly in the darkness, Roy sensed a presence. Glancing up, he was badly startled: not ten paces distant, a man watched them silently. Roy's stunned gaze fixed on the man. He wore butternut homespun over infantry boots. Under the Confederacy's flat cap, he leaned on a long muzzle loader. And there he stood, dead-silent, grinning at them.

For an instant, unsure of his own vision, Roy's thoughts flashed to the money in his trust. Deliberately he retrieved the revolver from his glove compartment and, making sure that the stranger could see him do it, he tucked the gun in his belt.

"What do you want?" He stared straight at the ragged figure.

There was no reply.

Now, the teaching profession requires an eye for detail and a keen memory, and Roy possessed both. "I can see him," he told me, "as plain as if it were yesterday. He stood there, leaning on that Kentucky Long Tom, just watching us and grinning with some secret joke.

"I thought I kept him in sight—he didn't move the whole time, and the tire took a good ten minutes. Then all at once, there was nothing there but the night. He hadn't walked away; I'd have seen it. He'd just disappeared. And we got out of there quick."

Several years would pass before Roy was certain of what had watched him at the old bridge. With San Antonio friends one evening, he met Lt. Colonel Scott Townsend, who had served as provost marshal at Camp Swift, near Bastrop, during World War II. The colonel knew of the apparition at the bridge; his knowledge had come in the line of duty.

During the early war-training years, a number of Camp Swift men, crossing that bridge at night, had seen the thing. Sightings became numerous; Townsend had gone to look for himself, and it had met him. At that point the chief of military police investigated in detail: interviews were many, recorded testimony voluminous.

What had watched Roy all that dark time seemed confirmed as a long-dead Confederate trooper. He had been one of two brothers whose home was close by and who had volunteered early, both boys swearing that no matter how long or bloody the war, they would return home. Though only one brother survived, it would seem that both had kept their promise.

Now I'm not at all sure that you will glimpse or hear the grieving mother or come upon the grinning phantom at the bridge. I found no one in San Marcos who admitted to a more recent confrontation.

It may be that the long-ago bedsheet-shrouded boys produced the specter that so many saw when night fell on this deep timber.

I learned to never talk about bedsheet ghosts around Professor Roy Pennycuick. As I noted, he had a careful eye and a steel trap memory: he knew what watched him for ten silent minutes that lonely autumn night.

He didn't talk about it much, but he must have wondered, as doubtless did the investigating MP chief, why that dead Confederate trooper chose to stand guard in those months when World War II was closing in.

A warning about war to a new generation?

EDITOR'S NOTE: Professor Roy A. Pennycuick died in 2001 in San Antonio. He was a Professor of economics.

THE PROTECTOR

Marshall, Scottsville

In late December of 1968 Albert Agnor sensed a tornado brewing. Six miles beyond Marshall, driving hard, he skidded into the long, tree-lined drive that led to his home—in a dead heat with the fist of wind swinging at his home, his family within.

In the cyclonic torrent, a tree crashed in the road, barring the way. Before he could back up, a big cedar went down behind him. Blocked, Agnor could only watch and, in horror, await obliteration. How could he know that a friend, one who had preceded him in his century-old home, stood guard?

"Yonder, maybe a hundred feet to the west," he told me, "there were two pines, big ones. Then they were gone." We were standing where Agnor, a thickset man with keen, dark eyes, had been trapped that fateful day. He pointed eastward. "Pecans over there had their tops torn off. My fence was leveled." His flat drawl reflected honest amazement. "All hell, on both sides of the house!"

Yet directly before him, the little porch-mounted hurricane lanterns, Christmas candles still within, remained undisturbed. Not one roof shingle flew. Serene and untouched, his home awaited him. Incredibly, this tornado had split and passed to either side.

In the morning, Mamie Evans, the woman who had tended the Agnor home longer than anyone could remember, called. She knew the storm had aimed for it, and wanted to check in. "Nothin' hurt the house, did it?" she asked Mrs. Agnor, going on to declare, "Mr. Lattimer, settin' up on top, jus' ain't gonna let it. An' he gets Help. The Good Lord *knows* that man!"

From that day onward, Albert Agnor knew of him, too. Clifton Lattimer, by then sixty years dead, was his friend.

"I can't refute what I saw happen," said Agnor. "Just this close, that tornado split."

To understand Mr. Lattimer's attachment to the Agnors, we go back to the days when neighboring little Scottsville was full of plantations, and its Scott family—a big one—sought to recover from the Civil War. Francis Marion Scott took eight years building this home and, shortly after completing it in 1879, he died.

To the family's dismay, his widow married again, and Clifton Lattimer at once became a man whom the Scotts would not accept. To them he was not only an intruder but, upon the death of his wife, his single-handed management of the old place was unthinkable.

Despite the shunning from his new family, Lattimer tried hard to get along. He kept this house in good condition, even improved it, but not one of his wife's kin would set foot inside, not even her grandchildren.

He built a gristmill and a second mill for lumber. He constructed a third mill for making syrup. On Sundays he would head for Marshall to sell his produce.

In the early 1920s, the rejected recluse died. The property passed from family hands and fell into disrepair. For more than two decades to follow, folks in Marshall and Scottsville heard talk of an irascible ghost that roamed the old place.

"If left alone, help wouldn't stay," Agnor said. "He'd scare 'em, laughing and calling after them when they ran. They'd start out the door, and there he'd be, sitting in that big magnolia tree."

In 1951, Elizabeth Ann Agnor, a stepdaughter of one of the builder's grandsons, and Albert took the place, determining to restore it. From that moment on, things began to change at the plantation. Lattimer was no longer seen. There was a sense that he was trying out the new owners. I suspect that Mr. Lattimer may have found Agnor a hard man to dislike. He had a countryman's feel for the land, and he was a traditionalist who respected the old ways. He operated a successful insurance agency with the élan of a cracker-barrel whittler, and his consuming love was the concoction of chili—he won both the San Marcos and Terlingua cook-offs and marketed it widely; it is still available to this day under the Albert Agnor's Championship brand.

Easygoing, contagiously friendly, and respectful of the past—score three Agnor points with Clifton Lattimer!

Then the home restoration: from furnishings to etched glass front door, as near the original as the Agnors could achieve. In the simple, white Greek Revival that overlooks wooded Millstone Farm, the Lattimer handiwork revived. Another good mark!

"Finally," Agnor reflected, "we've always been a very close family, something I reckon he missed. Maybe he just decided to join up."

From the beginning, the family was aware of an unseen presence: lights winked on and off, doors opened and closed, household items disappeared.

"Mr. Lattimer must have figured they were out of place," Agnor thought. "I remember one cut glass bowl I brought home: he didn't make off with it. He broke it.

These minor instances were forgotten after the times Lattimer was able to show his fondness for the house and its inhabitants in the storm.

"The one in sixty-eight, the way I saw it split . . ." Agnor shook his head. "Ten years earlier, we'd had another one. Not as bad, but it tore up things around us, and it seemed to have just circled our place. Of course, back then we laughed at Mamie Evans when she started in about Mr. Lattimer's sitting on the roof."

He led me into the broad, shaded backyard and paused under a large pecan tree not far from the house. In 1964, at the foot of the tree, he was repairing a pump when a thunderstorm came lashing.

"Elizabeth Ann was in the doorway, calling me in, when the lightning struck the very top." Agnor pointed toward an erratic sear, far down the dark bark to a knob directly over our heads. "It should have fried me," he said slowly. "But right above my head, that lightning shot out of the yard, horizontal to the ground."

I wondered aloud if it was the protective hand of Clifton Lattimer.

"Oh, I always looked for a logical explanation." Again, he grinned. "Now, that split tornado four years later. After that, I just quit looking."

The old house, he told me, had a widow's walk atop the roof, and it was up there that Mr. Lattimer always took station to look out over his land. High there, Mamie Evans had insisted, is where the old gentleman stood guard when trouble came.

Nearer the house, Agnor halted us beneath one of the mightiest pecans in this state. Along its side, as far as I could see, lightning had stripped a pale, four-inch-wide scar, top to bottom. Flourishing, the great tree ignored it.

"That was April of this year," Agnor said. "It should have knocked a ton of that tree right onto our roof. Instead, it stripped a little bark." He pointed at the base. "Yet right there, it dug a hole bigger than a washtub. A mighty big bolt!"

Out front, he recalled the big magnolia, the one Mr. Lattimer would climb to frighten Mamie Evans. One bolt had struck the crotch where the old man's spirit liked to sit. The tree was unscathed. In all, as Agnor summed it, two tornados and three near-hits from lightning. An untouched home; an unscathed family.

"Of course, I guess you could explain these things." He chuckles in a manner that leaves you unsure how far he's pulling your leg. "And I sure don't want to be superstitious. At A&M we had an inscription on a chemistry building that said education was supposed to free a man from superstition. I'd like to think I got my money's worth over there. But then, Mr. Lattimer . . ."

Had the old gentleman ever let them hear his voice, I asked?

"Oh, the night before our son, Stuart, married: August, this year," he replied. "Sounded like the old man was grieving. Like I said, we've been a close family, and now one of us would be leaving this home."

Shortly I, too, was leaving. Down the long drive that has always been there, I took a last look at the classic white home that the Agnors have revived, and that Mr. Lattimer shields. Well, why shouldn't he protect it? Why shouldn't he grieve when part of his family leaves home?

Maybe I really shouldn't have included this story. After all, Millstone Farm's fine old house isn't truly haunted. Instead, the Agnors have a somewhat unusual friend who happens to live with them.

THE NORTH BEDROOM

Austin

You wonder what Melissa really saw and heard when, with her closest girlfriend—both some sixteen years of age—she tried to face an entire night in that room. Could she not conceive that the dead man might be waiting?

Daughter of the Mansion's most faithful retainers and long at home there, Melissa knew the mounting tragedies that had beset those of this once-proud household. They were gone now. Everyone had left, it seemed. Everyone but Melissa's parents. To stay with this house was a duty they accepted.

Once so grand to Melissa, the Mansion seemed shabby now, one room charred from fire, the others shadowy with neglect and abandonment. As most of Austin did, the girl knew that Confederacy in Texas was near death, just as was its governor, already in the saddle for Mexico.

But it was the death in that upstairs north bedroom that had challenged the two girls to spend one night there. In the bed, close beside flickering firelight, they huddled as midnight loomed black at the windows.

Did they hear the creak of the opening door? The last awful groan of despair or death . . . or both? Or was it the sharp *click-clack* of a cocked revolver?

Could it have been what they saw? The frightful figure just above them by the bed? Did they see the pistol at his head? Or did he stand there, as dead as when he had sprawled, a brain-blown suicide, across the very bed where they lay?

That they ran screaming down the curving staircase is all we really know today: that, and the fact that no servant of this last Confederate household—including Melissa's parents—would again go near the north bedroom.

During the Civil War, Melissa had served in the great white brick mansion, stately today with its six Ionic columns and double galleries, altogether one of Texas's finest Southern Colonials and home to our governors for well over a century. Tradition suggests that Mirabeau Lamar selected the splendid site for the seat of the empire he envisioned.

In 1853, with Texas in the Union, the state's fourth governor, Elisha Pease, began construction on the Mansion, which would expand or modify with the style of the time and the taste of successive first families. The James Stephen Hoggs papered the walls; the Thomas M. Campbells terraced the front lawn. The Oscar Colquitts and Pat Neffs built additions. In the marble fireplace of the downstairs Green Room, old story insists that Sam Houston—hating secession—still burned a letter from Lincoln just before the Civil War.

Which brings us to the tragic two-year span beginning in 1863 when this was home to Texas's last Confederate governor, Pendleton Murrah.

Murrah was a South Carolinian who, in Texas, was an uncompromising States Righter, opposed to government centralism, whether US or Confederate. As the Confederacy's impending collapse began to show in printing press money, dollar postage for undelivered mail, shortages, wild inflation, and mounting home-front violence, he foresaw the end for Texas independence as well.

"In many sections," he told his last legislature, "society is almost disorganized, and the voice of law a dead letter. Whole communities live under a reign of terror and rule of the mob and the bandit."

There had been mass hangings along the Red River, deserter executions toward the coast, a near troop mutiny at Galveston, and Native assault sweeping almost to Fort Worth. And Pendelton Murrah, wracked with tuberculosis, knew himself a dying man. In the end, he would choose his grave in Mexico.

Under such all-engulfing doom, then, how could this mansion recall a solitary tragedy within its own walls? In the little north bedroom, a young man had drawn his pistol and put it to his own head . . .

Although documented, his story is understandably shrouded. In 1864, even while Texans were beating back invasion from Louisiana, the young man had arrived at the Texas White House. The identity of the man varies depending on who tells the story. In general, he is nineteen when he dies; he is either the nephew of the governor or of his wife, Sue Ellen. In some versions, he is just an acquaintance of the family.

Already visiting was a niece of Mrs. Murrah's, and the boy fell hopelessly in love. More, he must have been certain—so the story goes—that she returned his love. But when he asked her to marry him, her response was one of confusion. They had just been flirting harmlessly, she thought. Marriage was not in the cards.

It was near midnight when, a slow step at a time, he went up the winding staircase and into the small bedroom.

"That night," the *Austin Statesman* would recount, "the household was awakened by the pistol shot, and the poor fellow's body was found thrown across the bed of the little north room. The blood-spattered wall told the story."

Those stains yet remained when, as Union troops began to take control of Texas, the dying governor rode with other leaders for Mexico, and his anguished wife returned to her family to face reconstruction in Alabama. Of the servants, Melissa's family remained. Someone had to.

But something else remained as well, Melissa told them. Let them never enter that north bedroom!

The Mansion's next tenant, Governor A. J. Hamilton—a Texan who had fought in blue—knew the north room too. The servants tasked with cleaning the still-bloodstained walls refused to enter the room and fled.

Hamilton, in exasperation, sealed the room. It would remain that way for decades.

With all its blue uniforms and new faces, Austin may have spread the story faster. At midnight, strange things happened up there—for one thing, the awful sounds. If you'd known battle-smoke, you sure enough recognized the groans of a dying man.

And there was more: ask the men who'd worked there and quit. That door opened and closed with no visible hand near it. And stoke that fireplace as hot as you like, you could not rid the room of its cold.

The tales persisted through the 1920s; in 1925, when Miriam A. Ferguson sought her first governorship—a woman, mind you, and opposed to the Ku Klux Klan—the political trail buzzed. The Murrah ghost surely would be waiting for her!

In recent times the room has been repainted a soft white, and has been made part of the governor's private quarters. Every first family inescapably has known of the Mansion's other inhabitant. Rumors persist that Governor Murrah may also roam the halls.

Some may ask, "What then? Does the young man still haunt the room?" Consider the dilemma facing an honest ghost-hunter.

Suppose you approach a governor from the great state of Texas. Now suppose, you ask that governor if their home is haunted.

How does that person respond?

It could be noted that not too far from the Mansion, the shaded and hilly parts of old Austin were once graced with other fine homes, which knew ghosts of their own. Nearly all are gone now—the Raymond, Houghton, and House homes—and in their places modern pavement, concrete, and brick prevail. The splendid old Neill-Cochran House still stands on San Gabriel, but its once vast estate is now shoulder-to-shoulder with the university campus.

Those specters have nowhere to return to.

EDITOR'S NOTE: The Mansion, most often referred to as the Governor's Mansion in Austin, hosts other spirits. It is said that Sam Houston haunts the bedroom that he slept in. A large mahogany four-poster bed he bought still sits in the room.

It was not long after his death that reports began to surface of Houston being seen in hallways. A light above his portrait turns itself on as well.

Houston was forced out of office by the Civil War because he refused to swear loyalty to the Confederate States of America (CSA). Many assume it is because of this disgrace that he returns to this day.

THE CRYPTS OF OLD WAVERLY

Old Waverly, New Waverly, Evergreen

Like so many nights over Mrs. Walker's years in this old cabin, the ghosts have risen about her. Lights turn on and off, footsteps trace the attic, there is tapping at the walls, shrill whistles call from the darkness outside.

Despite this, she has been able to drift into slumber. She knows what roams the gloomy forest all about and, having been told by psychics that she possesses their sensitivity, she has not panicked, as have so many others who tried to live here. Yet, there is a certain dread in waiting for what is to come out of the night again . . . and again.

She has waked once, feeling cold breath on her neck, and in the twilight of returning sleep, she has seen—painted in her mind—a stark old wagon wheel, and she has heard a solitary fiddle, lonely with some antique tune unknown to her.

She will wake once more, deep in the night. Insistently clear, something is tapping her water glass on the bedside table. Restlessly she turns and, against the far, moonlit window, an opaque form—possibly more than one—glides away.

Since she will not frighten away, they will not allow her to rest.

To her astonishment, the next day while in town shopping, one store displays a record, its cover the painted wagon wheel that came in her dreams. That evening she will play the album, the final tune unmistakably the fiddle from the night before. *Soldier's Joy*, a Civil War-era tune ...

Old Waverly, itself a ghost, is hard to find. The Civil War destroyed its plantation way of life, and the railroad ended the town itself. New Waverly, on the other hand, is easy to find, just off I-45 about fifty-five miles north of Houston.

While not on a map, Old Waverly can be found ten miles to the east of New Waverly, the only markers an old graveyard and a church. Many still talk of this place as haunted ground.

To the northeast is Phantom Hill, where a headless creature stalks the night.

Southwest some forested miles is the cabin of Mrs. Walker, where three Federal soldiers were possibly entombed beneath the floor, and, since then, have driven away all who tried to live there.

Who were these soldiers? They were the occupying Federal troops who camped the little knot still called Soldier's Hill. Their objective was explicit: slavery must be ended, the plantations with it.

That some who camped Soldier's Hill and its small patrolling outposts would die as well is hardly surprising to any who penetrate these shadowed deeps. It is still land tangled enough to hide any sharpshooting rifleman.

"'Yellow fever,' I think they called it," one man told me. Forget his name; he's Old Waverly family and runs a store near where the town once prospered. "It killed a number of them." Death could be the more contagious, he admitted drily, the farther a trooper strayed from Soldier's Hill.

How far these strayed—there was a temporary camp near the Walker cabin—is not clear. You can be an intruder even to the living in this forest. They are as reticent as one must be when he thinks he knows what dwells beside him.

Lana Hughes Smith was one who thought she knew. A reporter as determined as any running back, the only way to write about ghosts, she believed, was to hunt them out.

She allowed the crypts of Waverly to rest, and she protected identities. Those of such close encounters are entitled privacy. It was at her direction that I've kept Mrs. Walker's real name secret.

Smith found the Walker cabin down a long, shadowed lane, a narrow one that must be little changed from the mid-1880s, when the cabin was built. The great, moss-hung trees press in upon it and upon its tiny cemetery, a short distance farther down. She found on its hillock a forebodingly gray and dilapidated house with a strangely masculine character. To her, despite its sagging age, it stood intangibly strong, defying anyone to abuse or disrespect it.

There was one night, she had learned, when the cabin's windows flashed gunfire, killing three Federal troopers, supposedly "mistaken for Indians." The death of the troopers was kept quiet: their entombment was immediate—under the cabin floor. No record exists on why these men were targeted. Rumors persist that they were responsible for the death of a young girl. Or, at the least, were held responsible.

Yet the dead were not silenced. From that time on, those who tried to live in the cabin stayed briefly. There was whispered talk of inexplicable noises, movement, a terrible gasped-out hacking cough, occasional glimpses of something that loomed in the darkened dwelling. One woman left the place mid–nervous breakdown. Those who preceded the Walkers tried to operate a dairy; they never remained after sunset.

The Walkers, on that ground for many years, would not yield . . . not entirely. They finally built a new home back-to-back with the original and lived there relatively undisturbed. They left the old home alone: a hostile presence remains, parapsychologists advise. Even in bad weather, the old cabin door left open, the Walker dogs and cats stand in the rain rather than go near that open door.

And so on two separate nights, Lana Hughes Smith stayed through all the dark hours in Mrs. Walker's old bedroom. She had brought all the necessities for good reporting: cameras, tape recorder, and companions to verify what might be experienced.

"There were some noises," she told me.

Others elaborated. There was a whistle, like the one Mrs. Walker heard. One of the men heard the fiddler. Another waked once to see the chair by the window rocking on its own. Two of the girls lay awake, each thinking the other had some kind of cough. Possibly they heard the cabin's death rattle.

"We tried to bring the Walkers' cat into the bedroom. Outside, she had been purring, but once inside that room, she fought to get out." To Lana, strangest of all was the fog: it rolled in dense, occupying the cabin's hilltop, yet the wind—fierce throughout the night—should have driven away any trace of mist.

"We didn't hear the drums and tramp of marching feet that so many have heard," she recalled. "But there were two screams. One was mine, when one of the others pulled at my foot. The other? It came from none of us. Two nights were enough."

Then what of Phantom Hill, about as far to the northeast as the Walker cabin hides southwest of Old Waverly? There, you need not fret about disturbing the dead; the hill's watchman seems to be waiting for you.

That sentry was probably most respected by Bob Janusch, a robust, outgoing young man who appeared ready for football when I spoke to him. He moved into the forest around nearby little Evergreen some years ago, and he projected an insatiable curiosity. What stalks that remote hill when night falls?

"I went up there one night with a friend," he told me. "We were hunting a hiking trail: there are some good ones in this forest. All at once I realized we had stopped on Phantom Hill. It was so dark, I didn't recognize it at first.

"Then I heard the thing coming," he said. "If you stop up there, it comes clumping through the trees and you can hear it, step by step. I told my friend to get out of there."

The friend apparently laughed and said, "You don't believe in that old story, do you?"

One old story insists that the hill's sentry was one who came to put down Old Waverly and strayed too far. Another simply tells of a newcomer who set up a sawmill and decapitated himself, falling into its teeth. Those who think they know what happened to the men of Soldier's Hill simply shrug.

"You bet I yelled at my friend," Bob Janusch recalled. "I heard the thing coming, and knew it could kill our engine." We got in the car, and then the engine wouldn't start . . . and here that thing came, step by step. We coasted, kicked into gear, and took off."

Bob Janusch went back more than once; Phantom Hill seems to draw him. Perhaps, like any of us who whistle past the graveyard, he has felt forced to prove his courage.

Deliberately one midnight, he pulled up on the rutted red crest. He surveyed the towering, close-crowding pines and for a moment, listened: there were only deep night sounds. Out of his pickup he stepped, and decided he would demonstrate the last word in man's defiance of peril from the unknown. Phantom Hill would be his restroom.

"And then he came," Bob said matter-of-factly. "Hell, it wasn't just hearing him this time; I could see something coming. I quit in the middle of everything, and if the car hadn't started, I'd have left it and run."

Would he care to show me the hill by night? Next time I came over, he would, Bob said. Tonight he was tied up. So alone, by watery daylight—it had rained for a week—I followed his map every mile of deep-rutted red mud.

No. I did not spend the night.

Atop Phantom Hill, turning around, I mired my camper to its hubs; it took a passing lumber truck to wench me out.

And, of course, lumbermen quit by dark. These left, and so did I.

THE FORETELLER

Lubbock

There is deep jungle looming far ahead. It will soon flash beneath, beyond the speed of sound. Hidden there will be the enemy, though he has safely traversed this area many times. A long veteran of combat, he knows the apprehensions that ride any flight over enemy territory. It has become commonplace.

Despite the normalcy of the flight, there comes a nagging voice in his head warning him that this time will be different. "Don't go straight in!" The voice will not leave him be. It is insistent. Why this feeling of danger? "Don't go straight in! This once, come out of the sun. Blind them to your plane!"

Suddenly compelled, he thrusts his Phantom Jet straight for the sun. A hunch, he thinks. Intuition. But it was much more.

At that time residing far from Vietnam was the most amazing of women. Helen could tap into a form of understanding few of us can even think about. Understandably, she preferred this to be known only to a select few; otherwise, the faddists and overcurious would engulf her.

For Helen, a quietly composed woman with intent blue eyes, this pilot's jungle passage—the barest eyelash from death—had been foreseen for many days. Visions of it began with a phone call from the East coast, the caller one of her closest friends.

Night after night, the friend's dreams had witnessed every terrible detail of her husband being shot down in Vietnam. It had become unbearable.

Step by step they retraced the dreams. Helen memorized their unchanging pattern until she too saw the enemy sky and forest. Then she sought her level of meditation, of openness. Some speak of drawing upon a "universal mind," of karma. Helen believes this direction comes directly from God. She refers to her work as "mind control."

Now she had to foresee that flight, envisioning an altered pattern that would escape death. She had to reach for the distant pilot, a difficult endeavor because—a close friend, too—he was skeptical of thought transference, or of any field explored by psychics. Still, like a television image beamed by satellite, Helen projected what she calls a "protective shield of thought."

"Very soon you will fly over jungle, a sector you've crossed before. This time they will be waiting; fly down on it, out of the sun." She could see the jungle now. Her vision pushed the plane toward the sun, then down its blinding shafts. There, indeed, was the glisten of sunlight on metal, hidden in the trees!

"You will see that glint. See them before they see you! You will get them before they get you—the guns or the rockets. Fly out of the sun!" Day after day she projected the warning. She had called the distant wife: her husband would be safe.

Later, he came home, decorated for his feat. Out of the sun, this once, he saw the warning glisten of new emplacements and—with their immense stores of ammunition—blew all of the hidden installation.

Homeward, he stopped in West, Texas. Did Helen know anything of a recent experience of his? As she spoke, he nodded, no longer skeptical. Already he had recognized his "hunch" as her voice transmitting across the thousands of miles.

I visited with Helen for a few hours in her comfortable home. A statuesque woman, pretty in her middle years, a tranquility surrounded her life and was reflected in her face.

"God places everything here for good," she said. "If we learn to use the mind given to us—*for good*—we can achieve healing, our personal goals, and our happiness. In mind control, I go from *what is* to what I wish the future to be . . . *within God's will.*"

For Helen, healing was the paramount motivation. She had been a registered nurse, an Air Force widow, and finally, a psychic. A most careful one.

She believed there are branches in our individual roads, and—within Divine Will—they can be open to our selection. Continual study and disciplined practice of mind control can often prevent unhappy eventualities. Or can prepare one for the unpreventable.

Quite apart from this story, yet important to it, is the fact that during our visit she startled me with several revelations regarding the lives of my family—matters of which no advance knowledge was possible.

Helen came upon her latent sensitivity as a young farm girl near Stamford, north of Abilene. She could anticipate the telephone's ring and its caller—intuition, she then thought. By degrees and over time, the "intuition" sharpened.

The turning point for her came when she had extreme difficulty with her pregnancy. In meditation, she envisioned the birth of a healthy son, the delivery, and the child himself.

Precisely as foreseen, the birth occurred, and Helen became a student of her abilities. Later she delved into formal study, reading all that she could.

She could foretell marriages before anticipation by anyone. She foresaw a friend's tragic accident—a wheel spun off the car—and by every indirect method possible without ever pretending to "play God," convinced the friend to have the car inspected, and the thread-held wheel was secured.

In the hilly little city where her two sons grew to bicycle age, she could summon them home by suggesting their thirst. Immediately they banged through the door for a drink of water. By degrees she could reach (if the need were valid) those who had died. She was called in consultation by the courts: in her mind control classes, the interest of attorneys had been aroused.

Again and again she was called upon to describe, to locate, to seek motive. Over the years she identified cars, occupants, and precise license plates. But her inclination was always to reach for the hunted man, to turn him from violence, to give himself up.

Once she reached a man who held his wife hostage at gunpoint. "You don't want this," she insistently projected to him. "You want to give yourself up without hurting anyone."

"I think that's what he did," she reflected. "Something went wrong in the way he did it and the officers shot him. I won't work criminal cases anymore."

Helen made no attempt to know whether she was the trigger to or the foreteller of what lay ahead. Perhaps this was due to her foreknowledge of her own husband's death.

Their station had been in Florida—he flew reconnaissance flights. Her husband sought a transfer homeward, to Reese Air Force Base in Lubbock; he had achieved everything life could give him except again flying the skies of his home state. First there was joy in returning to Texas, then one day she saw her first "picture" on the wall—"like a TV screen out of focus." But its "voice" was clear: joy would be short-lived. Her husband would die there.

Frantic, Helen tried every logical dissuasion—"you dare not state that you've foreseen death. . ." The more she objected, the more resolute her husband became. She turned her rejection to the eventuality itself: "I can't handle it. It simply can't happen!"

This telepathic battle she fought through the early days in Lubbock, flight after flight—young jet pilots in her husband's care.

"Finally he took one cross-country flight, and I knew this was when it was to happen. Minute by minute, I fought it. It didn't happen . . . and I was a wreck."

"Then one day when I was ironing, a profound sense of peace came over me, and I knew. Out loud, I said, 'Lord, I can accept it. Thy will be done.'"

Shortly thereafter, the Air Force classified a "freak accident." Over Tahoka, westward, a sand hill crane—far higher than they usually fly—struck the windshield at its one shattering point, crashed through and killed Helen's husband instantly. The other pilot landed the plane.

"To prevent what may be prevented," I was thinking to myself. "To prepare oneself for the unpreventable—for God's will."

In some ways the most dramatic of her telepathic outreaches occurred with another friend's husband, another fighter pilot over Vietnam. This time again, the awareness of impending disaster—a mind picture—was projected to Helen. How to tell someone, "I've just seen your husband shot down."

With great difficulty she remained silent, projecting shielding thoughts, finally sensing that he would come home safely. Then he did come home on leave, and Helen—still silent—relaxed.

That respite was premature. The pilot returned overseas and shortly word came that he was missing in action. Now she went to her distraught friend: he could not be dead. They must work together to reach him.

"Every day, I sought my level, and reached for him," she said. "Then one day I was in a dentist's chair, waiting alone, when his picture came on the wall, as sharply as any photograph. He spoke to me: 'Helen, I'm all right; I've hurt my leg and my back, but I'm all right.'"

From a crowded Vietnam prison compound—the pilot later would disclose this—he had reached for her. If his presence could get through to anyone, it must be Helen.

"I could see the prison buildings," she said, "a pinkish purple unlike any color we use, a kind of claylike brick. I could see him and the others, even the enemy guards." Yet inquiry after inquiry brought the standard Air Force response: missing in action. It was hard to convince his wife that he was safe.

Helen paused her story momentarily. She could tell I was accepting this. "I began to picture things as they could resolve themselves happily. I saw him boarding a homeward-bound plane, saw his guards determining to release him, saw his arrival in the States." Obviously she was looking back. "That was every day, for weeks. All that time, he seemed nonexistent."

She was en route for a visit to Iowa when something compelled her to stop for a newspaper, to turn far back to a small item: three American soldiers had been released, no reason given. She expected the phone call—the missing pilot's wife. Her husband was coming home.

"Were you willing the guards to release that man?" I asked her. "Or were you simply foreseeing what was to happen?"

"I don't know," she said. "Sometimes I think I'm allowed to be the 'trigger,' sometimes only a foreseer." She gestured. "There's so much we *don't* know about this field. Anyhow, lots of others have done much more than I. And we *do* know the field exists."

They knew this, centuries ago, when you think about it. There were the prophets who foretold what would be Scripture. In 1620, the visions of Maria de Agreda, a lovely young nun who never left her convent in the Spanish mountains, described in precise detail much of the Southwest, from New Mexico to East Texas, the Texas area then unexplored by Spain.

"The Lady in Blue" to Natives whom she taught Christianity was a miracle worker to her church—so much so that, in historic fact, she brought about the establishment of the entire Texas mission system. A miracle indeed.

And so it is that this psychic, Helen—who saw what was to be, or could be, as well as what had been—saw her experience in sound perspective. With disciplined release, she exercised her mind into fields opened to her by the Creator of her mind. This was no special "gift."

"With training, study, and dedication," she said, looking me in the eye, "*you* could do it. If it's for good, anyone can—it's a power open to all of us who will really try."

A wonderfully miraculous thought! To this power, we give man-conceived words like "mind control" but also "prayer" and "faith."

I must try harder.

THE HEADLESS HORSEMAN

Ben Bolt, San Antonio

The man was neither first nor last to see the headless horseman but, more than most, this man met it close, very close. And he would never forget it.

A sense of dread waked him. What was it—the nicker of his hobbled horse? A quick whisper of wind? Something was coming on his dark camp, very near in the scrub along the riverbank.

Silently he crawled into the cover of the cedar clump by his bedroll. He slid his Spencer repeater up and sighted into the night. Then he saw it.

Across the dark stream, the big mustang drank, pawing at the ground. Gaunt in the thin moon, his rider waited, leaning on his saddle horn with all the patience of death. But something was wrong. Even in this faint light the man could see the stump above his shoulders where a head should be. His head—its sombrero still secured—was swinging gently at his side, tied to his saddle horn.

The mustang finished drinking and headed across the stream right for him.

And the man fired for the thing's chest. The mustang reared, then came plunging on. The man levered two fast shots, sick with knowing that the first could not have missed. The horse ran into the darkness, its rider's head bouncing at its side.

This was more than a century ago, so the man's name is not that important: he was only one of many confronted by the headless horseman, that creature which stalked the brasada south and west of San Antonio. To understand what was seen, we must consider three graves, widely separated.

One lies within the old state cemetery in Austin. Secluded from the near-passing expressway, Texas Ranger Bigfoot Wallace rests. Another is in the tucked-away Knoxville graveyard just north of Kerrville. Here lie the mortal remains of Creed Taylor, sometimes ranger, sometimes outlaw. Creed and Bigfoot were friends.

An indistinct stone in La Trinidad's rancho cemetery marks the third in tiny Ben Bolt, below Alice, in the brush. Three graves removed from one another now, yet irrevocably bound together in history.

Call the third grave Vidal's: Creed Taylor did in his memoirs, although that wasn't really the man's name. Vidal came from a good family, but he had a fancy for other men's stock, and on one crisp fall morning in 1845, he selected a string of Taylor's horses and drove them down from the hills. Therein, the rustler erred: Creed was a tracker, as skilled as any Comanche.

Creed and a friend named Flores picked up the trail and followed it down along the Nueces. Where the river bends east below Uvalde, they ran into Bigfoot Wallace, who joined the hunt. It was high time to get that outlaw! The three rode hard into the night and came out on the bedded-down camp of their quarry. Only one guard paced drowsily.

Downwind, not to spook the dozing herd, they were so close to the camp that its waking men stumbled to their feet only to die in the sights of the trackers. One of the dead was Vidal.

Vidal had rustled from the border to the hills, and there was a price on his head, but Bigfoot had other plans. He cut the head from the outlaw's body. The trackers selected the wildest mustang in Taylor's stolen string and lashed the headless body in a saddle to the mount, binding the corpse's hands to the saddle horn. Then they worked a rawhide thong through the jaws of the decapitated head and tied all of it—sombrero, too—to the mustang's pommel. Then they cut the maddened pony loose. For a desperate time the horse fought his rider, but that grisly one was up to stay. The three avengers saw it as a warning to rustlers. The mustang broke for the horizon and beyond, into legend.

Quickly, those who rode the South Texas brush learned of El Muerto del Rodeo, the wandering dead man whom one dared not face. For an indeterminate number of years, this phantom panicked the lonely reaches from below San Antonio to the border. Troopers from Fort Inge, at today's Uvalde, saw him and retreated. Ranchers, vaqueros, and solitary travelers shuddered when they told of what had ridden down on them.

Many say that the horse and rider roamed until the sad animal died of old age. Horses can live up to twenty years, so the sightings were numerous. The body of the horse and Vidal were finally found near Alice. Vidal's body was a mummy by this time, as well as a sieve from bullet holes. They buried what was left at Rancho La Trinidad near present-day Ben Bolt, where surely it must rest today.

Or does it?

Northward, across Lake Corpus Christi from Mathis, is the old ghost town, Lagarto. Almost two centuries ago this was a Mexican settlement, by the 1860s a promising town. Throughout its life, the old ones there could tell of an evil horseman who rode the night. It was better only to hear—never see—him pass.

Up near West, above Waco, such a rider still warns a ghost ranch of impending massacre. Near San Diego, when the moon is down in Duval County, a decapitated ranchero still races beside Dead Man's Lagoon. To the northeast at old San Patricio, is Headless Horseman Hill, where a phantom rider has driven his spectral mount through at least one terrified wagon team.

None of these is Vidal. In such a tortured grave, why then should he rest? Besides, as Seguin's Charley Eckhardt puts it, Creed Taylor could stretch the blanket a bit when telling his stories. Bigfoot was notorious for it as well. Charley, who could ride or shoot or, for that matter, write of old Texas as well as anybody, questioned getting a dead man astride a wild mustang. Though a point worth pondering, it does not dismiss this story.

Some time ago, I stopped at a wayside service station / grocery between San Diego and Benavides, deep in the brush. Had anyone really heard or seen this horseman?

The man behind the counter gave a tolerant shrug reserved for those of age and the wisdom that grows from it.

Oh, yes. He knew of the grave near Ben Bolt.

And I thought, everybody can be buried, but no one said the body had to stay put.

THE HOUNDS OF OROZIMBO

Orozimbo

The once-great, moss-draped Orozimbo Oak is listed among Texas's most famed trees. And, to the uncurious perhaps, roaming the lonely forests just above the little lakes and twelve miles northeast of the old colony town, the sight of three dogs watching from the shadows may not be singular.

But should you happen upon them, look closely. They are a strange off-white in color, two of them shaggy, the other seeming almost raw in appearance. They make no sound and may disappear as you watch. Perhaps you saw their glazed eyes? You see, these dogs have been here for almost a century and half.

I learned of this story from Catherine Munson Foster's *Ghosts Along the Brazos* (Texian Press, 1978), a book whose small size belies the skill of its storyteller. Though long out of print, copies can be still be found.

Around old West Columbia, in the southeastern coastal forests of the Brazos River, only a secluded cemetery plot remains at what was Orozimbo. The great plantation of Dr. James Aeneas E. Phelps, one of Stephen F. Austin's original colonists from Mississippi, was destroyed in a 1932 hurricane. Phelps was a surgeon at San Jacinto, present when a wounded Sam Houston confronted Antonio Lopez de Santa Anna and defeated him in eighteen minutes.

What to do with this high-profile prisoner?

Kill him, was the verdict of those whose kin had fallen at the Alamo and Goliad. Fortunately, wiser heads prevailed. As a hostage, Santa Anna would ensure no further invasion and the negotiation of Texas independence. In Washington, President Andrew Jackson could mediate all this, Houston believed.

Yet where to hold the man? Velasco proved unsafe; he was shot at. Revenge-bent vigilantes blocked his ship at the mouth of the Brazos before it could depart for Washington. The general and his staff were taken prisoner and moved to nearby Columbia, but the hazards remained: an Alamo widow openly planned his execution.

Upriver from Columbia, Orozimbo was remote and comfortable. From July to November, 1836, Dr. Phelps was more host than jailer. Some twenty men guarded the possible guarantor of Texas freedom, but the notable prisoner could relax in a courteous sanctuary.

If lonely Orozimbo offered safety to Santa Anna, it also lay exposed to escape. Perhaps a daring rescue? One bold young Mexican officer had such a plan; he would sneak into the compound and break the exiled ruler from his prison. He selected a night that was cold and black with misting rain. The guards were lazy and bored with their duties and were ready enough for wine offered them by a mysterious prisoner whose unfamiliar appearance went undetected. Then there were no guards at all: the wine had been drugged. The Phelps household, with all its retainers, fell into a deep slumber.

In the silence that only the small hours bring such a night, Santa Anna waited. Somewhere beyond the near edge of the forest, he knew his rescuers were coming.

Instead, out in the woods, a great chorus of growling dogs arose. The sound had swelled as though scores of dogs assailed the night in an outcry of grief and alarm. It is said that the rescue party ran away.

Of course, as history records, Santa Anna left Orozimbo finally to travel to Washington and, ultimately, to reach a peaceful recognition of Texas independence.

But what of the hounds that history overlooks? They were not a pack at all, protested the servant who had seen them after waking from his drugged slumber. There were only three. Strange, wild-looking things. Two, a strange unearthly white in color. The third one looked as if it had been skinned. Even in the dark he saw their milky eyes. Then they just faded away.

What, indeed, of those guardian hounds? For miles around, there was only empty forest. And at Orozimbo there were no dogs at all.

Not long afterward, a traveler stopped in Columbia and confirmed what the servant had seen, leaving an explanation that has persisted over the years.

He recognized the dogs' description. They had belonged to a neighbor up toward Washington-on-the-Brazos. He had never known a man who loved his dogs more or was so loved in return.

The only time those hounds had not followed their owner was at his refusal—when he went off to fight for independence. He was one of the 309 who fell at Goliad. Afterward, the dogs avoided the house, refused to eat, and finally disappeared into the woods.

Some of that man's friends believed they had gone searching. Some thought they must have turned wild. Just about everybody agreed that surely they had died. Strange, the traveler thought, that finally they would turn up all the way down here.

It had been such a long time since their master had been shot down at Goliad.

The sightings were always the same, and they were singular. These did not run like hunting hounds and a man did not so much *see* the dogs as he suddenly felt eyes watching him. Then, off in the shadows, the watchers could be detected—three of them, wild-looking, strange in color. There for a moment they were, then gone. But for that moment, a man would never forget the utter silence.

Those glazed-over eyes.

As the years turned, Orozimbo's hounds were seen from time to time, and old-timers began to debate. How could they be around so long? Unless...

According to Catherine Munson Foster, whose forebears helped settle that country, a man and his wife saw the dogs as recently as 1974. They were near the big oak and the lonely cemetery that is all that remains of Orozimbo.

Since I could find no one who would admit to having glimpsed them, I poked around that still-remote woodland for a time, but with little luck.

You might do better, and you can reach the old plantation site—given permission, for this is "no trespass" property—if you can maneuver an obscure combination of backroads that nudge along the lake-flanked west bank of the Brazos. You will find that the gap is generally locked, the last mile or so to be taken afoot. You follow a lane that leads into heavy timber.

I left at twilight. I had made out two whitetails and twice thought I saw something in the trees beyond the old cemetery, but when I looked closer—I'd left my glasses in the camper—nothing really was there. Walking back, I dismissed the feeling that something watched me go.

Now, if you should come upon them—I suspect it will be on the dark side of twilight. You'll know them by their eyes.

LADY OF THE LAKE

White Rock Lake, Dallas

Their lights dimmed, the young couple had parked near the north shore of White Rock Lake. They were oblivious to the gentle glint of water, even to the lights of Dallas, spread out beyond in the spring night.

The girl in white startled them, for she had seemed to appear from nowhere, all at once beside their Model A coupe. More, she was dripping wet, her evening gown like a second skin. There had been an accident. She must get home. She gave an address on Gaston Avenue in Dallas.

Would they help her? She was sorry to impose.

There was nothing to do, then, but pack the girl into the rumble seat and drive for the address she'd given. Occasionally they glanced back; it was not easy to see her at all times. The small rear windows of that era made rearward visibility difficult.

Slowing to make sure of the address—they were nearing it—this couple was astonished. Their lady of the night was gone. The rumble seat was wet: she'd been there, no doubt about that. She couldn't have jumped, the young man insisted; he had been driving too fast.

At the girl's address, an elderly man came to the door. Within the past month, they were the third to bring him the news. His daughter had drowned some weeks earlier in White Rock Lake.

Now, before you protest that the "Hitchhiking Harriet" story is an old one, known coast to coast, let me dismiss argument with agreement: I've encountered it across all of Texas. Near Henderson, northeastward, a girl rides homeward only to disappear. Far west, along the lonely stretches around Big Spring, there's another phantom companion, an accident victim, as is the case on an expressway near Waco. Far south near Benavides, a young man danced a night away with a lovely girl who, at midnight, left him for her grave. I am sure you know of others.

Yet there is something that sets the Lady of White Rock Lake apart.

Over the years, she has appeared at many homes along the northeast lakeshore, always in that skin-soaked white evening gown, always seeking help. She had lost control of the car. No, she wasn't hurt but . . . might she use the telephone?

Of course she might. But when the porch lights flood on, she has disappeared, only a tiny puddle of water to assure the witness that the girl really had stood there. Dallas of the 1920s and 30s knew her well.

One respondent, an East Texan who prefers anonymity, declares that he led her to the telephone and, out of courtesy, turned aside while she called her number. "I wasn't a half-dozen paces from her," he told me. "I kept telling myself I knew what she was, but she was too pretty and too real for me to believe it.

"I could swear I heard the phone ring at the other end of the line. Then someone picked it up and, when I looked around, the girl had vanished. Before that I was close enough almost to have touched her."

Mark J. McCarthy of Kermit is more explicit regarding the mysterious lady's background. "During the 1920s, White Rock was a popular recreation spot, and there was an excursion boat operating there. There was a dance band, a small dance area, and refreshments. It was a place to moderate the summer heat in the days before air-conditioning."

A Dallas man—some say a bootlegger—and his lady had been enjoying an evening on the boat and, on this occasion—the party was formal—they were both in evening dress. During that evening they had a terrible argument, and when the boat docked the lady ran from the deck, jumped into the man's car, and drove off.

The roads around the lake were quite poor at the time, and the lady may have been sampling too much of the refreshments. As she approached the area where Lawther Drive now joins Garland Road, she lost control of the car, and it plunged into the lake. She died in the accident. Her ghost is said to have two ways of manifesting itself. The most common is to appear as a hitchhiker along Garland Road where it passes the lake. The spirit materializes drenched in an evening gown. She gives a certain address but soon disappears. The lady has been known to leave her wrap in the car, this said to bear a 1920s-style Neiman Marcus label.

The other manifestation, according to McCarthy, is the emergency phone call, always delivered on the front porch of homes along Garland Road facing the lake.

"I've never seen her," McCarthy adds, "but friends of mine have said they saw her hitchhiking. They didn't stop. They didn't want to deal with a ghost."

My friend Charley Eckhardt of Seguin is an able writer, and we all know what embroidery able writers can stitch into any story. However, Charley is also an ex–North Dallas lawman, and when he talks of the Lady of the Lake, I write off nothing.

The occurrence involved his partner, Steve Wester, a big man who had time for little more than fact. Charley is quick to point out that this account declines to follow the "Hitchhiking Harriet" formula and, for that, Eckhardt places some credence on it.

Wester encountered the lady in the mid to late 1960s. Up around the north end of White Rock, up in the marshy area close to the Northwest Highway–Lawther Road intersection.

Charley continues his story. "It was quite late, and Steve had left his car, working with a flashlight, for something seemed wrong toward the water, and he went sloshing down to see about it. All at once he saw a woman, soaking wet, come walking out of the reeds at the lake's edge.

"There was nothing insubstantial or ghostly about her. She was apparently in her late twenties or early thirties.

"She walked straight at Steve, where he stood holding the light on the path. She walked directly past him, and it was then that Steve—even though he was a little shaken by it—asked if she needed help.

"She ignored him. He shined his light after her—she needed to see where she was going; it was pitch dark. Then it dawned on Steve that she was not leaving one single footprint behind her. And that ground was marshy enough to bog a kitten."

The White Rock Lady?

"I don't know," Charley says. Then, after a moment, adds. "I know she damn sure made a believer out of Steve Wester."

And out of you and me? Well, I'm no longer so quick to scoff at the Big Spring Lady, nor some of the others.

What do you and I know, anyway?

Let me suggest something to you, since I have begun to suspect—quite sensibly, I think—that ghosts may have the same motivations as people. Maybe she just wanted someone to help her find the way home.

THE SISTER

Austin, Utley

The pain was enough to blur the man's vision, but he could still see the naked Comanche squatting above him, the bloody knife in his hand, his focused yet indifferent manner as he went about this work of scalping.

This must not, could not, be happening! But what some outraged corner of his mind protested, the man's eyes could plainly see. Death had come for him.

He could scarcely feel the knife. There was a great tearing sensation and a sound like distant thunder.

Then nothing.

That Josiah Wilbarger was dead, along with the other two, the surviving two rangers were certain. The survivors had broken clear of the ambush, reached their horses and, sickened with the screams behind them, ridden to safety. By twilight they were within the log walls of Reuben Hornsby's fort, at the great bend of the Colorado on the east edge of today's Austin.

Yes, the others were all dead, they reported. Wilbarger was the last man scalped.

As night closed in, they could only recall—still shaken with the horror of it—how suddenly it had happened.

That at that moment in the gathering dark, something was still willing Wilbarger to cling to life, those rangers never could have imagined.

In this August of 1833, there was no village of Austin—only the deceptively gentle valley of the Colorado, the seeming tranquility of purple hills westward, and the log fort of Reuben Hornsby, the white man's most advanced outpost inside Comanche land.

Just downriver from where tiny Utley today strings along the old Webberville Road, Josiah Wilbarger's fort stood, guarded by its own river bend. The Kentuckian was Hornsby's nearest neighbor and his close friend, and the two frontiersmen had agreed to scout this splendid valley for a new Stephen Austin colony—a valley that Mirabeau Lamar would choose for Texas's capital seven years later.

And so on this mild summer morning and in the handsome strength of his thirty-two years, Wilbarger had led out his scouts. There were four others, frontiersmen all who, like himself, feared nothing.

Their trail followed a path that today leads from Webberville Road to the site of Austin's former Robert Mueller Municipal Airport. At its southeast edge, the group flushed a Comanche rider and trailed him north up Walnut Creek. In close timber, he escaped. They back-trailed along Pecan Springs Branch, and reined up in a heavy stand of oak. They hobbled their horses to take a meal.

Corn pone and jerky, then cold spring water to wash it down. What better meal for men vitally alive in magnificent country? They stretched to rest in the shaded quiet. But it was too quiet, and they should have known it.

Moments later, the ambushing Comanche attacked.

One man dropped, screaming. Another, his hip shattered, fell outside their fort of trees, and Wilbarger went after him. Instead, hit in both legs and in the throat, Wilbarger went down.

All three dead, the survivors were certain. They'd watched the Comanche swarming over their bodies. Yes, they would ride back, not to bring help, but to bury their friends.

That night Reuben Hornsby told his wife Sarah that by morning, help should ride in, perhaps enough to attempt a burial party. Now, he insisted, was not a time to dwell on what had happened; they must try to sleep while they could.

But Sarah Hornsby could not sleep. A woman's voice, urgent, was whispering to her, would not leave her thoughts. So she waked her husband and told him what now seemed certain to her: that Willbarger was not dead; they could save him.

Hornsby hushed her. She must have been dreaming.

Later, she woke him again. Josiah Wilbarger was still alive, she said. He was lying against a live oak, naked and scalped. A voice had told her this, Sarah explained to her husband. The man had pulled a sock over his head to stop the bleeding. He was hanging to life. Waiting for them to come.

Eventually, Reuben Hornsby listened to his wife. Before first light, he had horsemen enough to risk a try.

Under the oak they found Wilbarger just as Sarah Hornsby had described, even to the bloody sock over his head, clinging to life. As gently as they could, they transported the dying man back to the fort.

For days, they treated his wounds and soothed his head with bear oil.

In the delirium of those first days, Wilbarger mumbled of his sister, Margaret. As he recovered, he became more certain—it was Margaret's voice that held him from the pit of death. And he told his story:

As twilight came, something waked him.

In his vise of pain, he realized he was alive, and that he was naked, all his clothing ripped away except for one sock. The Comanche were gone, and away in the dark hdl to protect it from the elements, and in desperation he tried to drag himself toward Hornsby's fort. He made it a quarter mile before collapsing against a live oak to wait for death.

But Margaret's voice would not leave him. "Hold on!"

Sarah Hornsby told Wilbarger of the voice that awakened her all through that same night. There was no question now; it was also Margaret, beseeching Sarah to send help in time.

Yet this was impossible. Margaret lived in St. Louis! Sarah and Josiah decided they must write, even if Margaret would never believe their story. But before they could pen the letter, within a day, a letter arrived from that distant city. Margaret was dead. She had died the day *before* her brother rode into ambush.

Josiah Wilbarger lived eleven more years. His wounds never fully healed and he wore a fur cap to protect the exposed parts of his skull. He died at his home near Bastrop in 1845 after hitting his head on an exposed support beam in his cotton gin. Wilbarger County is named for him.

EDITOR'S NOTE: Austin's Robert Mueller Municipal Airport (located in the northeastern central portion of the city) closed in 1999 and was replaced by the Austin-Bergstrom International Airport on the southeastern edge of town. The old airport is now the site of a residential development and a film studio.

THE DEVILS OF MILAM SQUARE

San Antonio

The figure swam before his eyes, wearing a cassock like the old padres, with the hood pulled over its face. Was it a face? Was that not white bone, a skull with black holes for eyes? And from far away, a muffled voice calling him . . .

"I have come for you, Felix Perez," the voice told him. "Are you ready for me?"

"I am not ready," he said, and shrank from the reaching hand.

He awoke in the emergency ward of San Antonio's Santa Rosa Hospital. He had been delirious. He had been shouting to be left alone, that he didn't want to go. He had a bad head wound. He would live, but he had experienced a close call.

Sinking back against the cold of the emergency table, Felix Perez knew it had been close indeed. And he knew something else: this had happened because he had forgotten to avoid the devils of Milam Square.

Next time, its devils would surely kill him.

Felix Perez had to depend on the long memory he had earned. In old age, eightyish and blind, he could still see the devils, which thirty years previously had risen from the graveyard that once lay near that plaza. How many times had they waited there to assail him?

Now, *this* San Antonian knows his city's history perhaps only in a general way, but he understands rightly that Milam Square is one of the old town's most ancient areas. Today it is flanked southward with El Mercado's intriguing shops, the market area that tourists love to browse. It was somewhat less tourista-oriented when Felix grew up. Then it was Haymarket Plaza or, in the close by neighborhood where he lived, La Parrian. There was a fine earthy smell, chili stands and little vegetable stalls and handcarts and, here and there, musicians with guitars or wise men who stood on boxes delivering profound speeches on all sorts of things—a place where one could also buy a splendid meal for fifteen cents. At night, it became even more exciting: beer flowed foamy, and anything could happen.

That was how Feliz Perez, not yet thirty, first met the devils.

"Of course, they are still there," he told me. "On dark nights when there's trouble. Where else?"

He and two friends had walked up San Saba Street toward Commerce, where an all-night place provided, for two dimes, a taco and a beer to wash it down. They already had enjoyed other beers and two near-fights, Felix admits, when the policemen stopped them. They were drunk, the chief officer asserted.

They were not drunk, Felix protested and prepared to resist, for even though he is short of stature, he was very strong.

The chief policeman grew angry, and Felix became frightened—not of the officer, but of what he saw behind the man.

"Something big was right behind him. He wore a kind of cape and helmet, and he grew bigger and bigger as the policeman got madder. You could see him, and yet you could see through him."

The three were arrested and jailed as drunks.

Yes, his friends had seen it, too. It was a devil, no doubt at all. A night or two later, Felix went back to see if the devil would return, but the creature did not appear. And so he tried to forget the matter.

Some months later, he was crossing Milam Square toward the old Teatro Nacional. Beside the newspaper office of La Prensa, a taxicab had stopped, and the driver was watching him. It was late, and very few people were about.

"Come over here," the driver called to him, and got out of his cab. Felix walked across. He wasn't afraid until two men jumped from the shadows. They demanded his money, and since he had just been paid, his wallet was full.

He backed against the dark wall of a building and drew his knife. Then he saw it—a hazy form that seemed to swell from the night behind the three men. It swelled larger and larger, like thick smoke, yet in the form of a giant furious man. A devil, Felix knew, and felt his knife hand trembling. But the men had stopped short.

They were staring at something *behind him*, looking higher and higher at something that must have been enormous. Then they broke and ran, and Felix turned. There was nothing behind him, nothing but the wall.

"I think there was a devil behind me," he said.

This time, the respite of Felix Perez was brief indeed. Another night found him crossing the square toward Produce Row. Two men stepped from the shadows of an alley. They had knives; it was another holdup.

Anger flooding Felix, he seized an iron bar and started warily toward those knives. To his astonishment, the men backed away, staring, and once again, toward something that loomed behind and above him.

"My God!" one of them yelled. They both ran.

I noted that the creatures seemed to feed on anger. My question was more direct, though: "Why do the devils appear only on Milam Square?"

"Oh," he said, "I am sure that they are in other places. But here is where they were buried in anger. It is how one is buried—angrily or peacefully—that determines one's temperament as a ghost."

Not long afterward, Felix sought the counsel of old and wise men, those who had known the great healer and prophet, Don Pedrito Jaramillo. Don Pedrito was a man of miracles who, in South Texas, was known as a sort of St. Francis.

In the very beginning, Felix would learn—the year was 1718— Spanish padres placed San Antonio's first little church very near where

Milam Square is located. There was a cemetery that grew in size as the Apache struck, and the Spaniard struck back: there was much evil killing. From here, buried deep, the evil could rise to any nearby person who let the thought of violence steal upon him. The city eventually removed the headstones, but left the graves intact.

Don Pedrito had spoken of other devil dwellings—closer to San Pedro Park and near the headwaters of the San Antonio River—but these did not concern Felix—he had asked only of Milam Square.

"Knowing why the devils are there," Felix told me, his sightless eyes intent on my face, "it was easy to make up my mind not to get angry when I was near that place . . . even if I always seemed to get in trouble there."

"Is it easy . . . " I asked carefully, wanting to follow his reasoning to its end, "for one of those devils to get inside a man?"

"All he has to do," Feliz answered quickly, "is to get mad."

For a long time, Felix Perez successfully resisted the devils of Milam Square. He visited about the place, filled only with goodwill. He had almost forgotten the old troubles when, in the 1950s, he took a job as a night watchman at the Santa Rosa Hospital.

One night, while seated on a bench facing the square, he saw a couple in the shadows of a building, and he heard the woman cry out. Then he saw the man with the gun and charged across the street.

"You're under arrest!" he shouted, running for the man, who was turning as Felix drew his own gun. It was then that something indistinct rose up—not behind the man, but directly between them. It had swelled to enormity as Felix tried to reach through its seeming substance to seize the man.

"Stop!" He heard a terrible hollow voice, and something struck his head, and then again. For a moment, he saw one of the devils above him, and then nothing. He did not know how long it was before he saw the other figure, the terrible one with a skull for a face, the one that reached for him.

But what of the robber?

"He ran," Felix said. "Maybe the devils knocked him down, too, because they sure caught him and put him in jail.

"Have you ever seen one of the devils since then?" I asked after a time. He placed a forefinger over each eye.

"I don't go to Milam Square anymore." He thought for a moment. "If I did, I would be very careful not to get mad."

EDITOR'S NOTE: El Mercado is the largest Mexican market in the US today.

THE ATTIC LODGER

Galveston

The attic stairway was a steep shadow at the end of the hall, and high up it, the big man hesitated for a long time. Below him, on the stairs, the reporter watched anxiously. What was behind the door?

Quickly, the man jerked the door open and stood facing the darkness. The reporter felt a blast of unnatural heat from above.

The man turned abruptly. "I can't go in there." He was sweating, his voice, hoarse.

Shortly, the man would vacate this house where, for only a brief time, he had been a tenant. What drove him from that house, and even the city itself, was the deadly hostility of another lodger, someone or something that dwelled in the attic gloom.

The house? It is one of Galveston's old Victorians, austerely tall, severe with gables and grayed with sea-worn age—a large house and forbiddingly strong, particularly to those who think they know some of its baffling genealogy.

Dick Bryant of the *Galveston News* was the reporter on that staircase, and in the 1975, he wrote of the events at the Mott House on Tremont, in the old part of the city.

For this story, though, I sought out Neal Witwer, a youthful-looking man with inquiring eyes and a restless nature. Although the attic lodger never came directly at him, it assailed his first marriage, and it set upon his friend—the man at the door.

Born in the house in 1947, Neal was old enough to know it, and young enough to puzzle over its past. It was natural then that Neal would be part of almost nightly séances—two weeks of them—held in the high-ceilinged room directly below the attic.

Neal occupied those quarters, reasonably untroubled by the dark above him. He simply avoided it. More, he suspected that only a strange set of circumstances—his first wife's name (we'll call her Kitty to protect her identity) and the physical appearance of the friend who was driven away—roused the attic lodger in the first place.

Built in 1884, the Mott House was bought in 1943 by Neal's father, Tommy Witwer. The Witwer Photographic Studios, together with another business establishment, occupied the first floor of the building during the time this story was told to me. From the studio one may pass directly into the old quarters, climb a balustrade stairway to a spacious second-floor hall, flanked on either side with great, tall rooms. To the left is the room where Neal and his first wife, Kitty, lived. Beyond are the attic stairs.

For all his life, the attic had intrigued Neal—a big, dusty, dark, cluttered place. His brother Joseph claimed to have seen a bearded figure near the stairs when they were younger. How could Neal suspect that something within the attic would be roused by Kitty's presence?

"I guess I should have known something was wrong," he told me, "when out of the blue, she asked me who 'the Captain' was. She couldn't know that a Captain Mott had built the house. Our family knew almost nothing about him, and she was new to Galveston."

Then Neal's young daughter began to speak of "the Captain," a nice old man who came into her room at night and wanted her to come live with him.

"I didn't even know," Neal confessed, "that my sister always insisted there were ghosts up there. She had only told my parents."

Then Kitty began to wake her husband, always around three a.m. Someone was moving things in the attic. Heavy things. Three times,

Neal climbed into the dark and came down irritated with her overactive imagination. Kitty responded with silence: shutting her experiences away from Neal until things reached the point of no return.

Neal would not be told that each time he left the room to climb the attic stairs, Kitty heard quick malevolent laughter. Nor would he be aware that shortly afterwards she caught a mirrored glimpse of a bearded man, something that vanished even as she gasped in fright.

Only toward the end would Neal learn of the wave of trances that began to overcome his wife. She would find herself, fully clothed, on the bed, beset by an inability to move. Then she would hear a voice: "It's all right; I'm here. I won't let anything happen to you." The voice called her Katherine, Kathleen, and finally, Kitty.

At the end, too, the couple would be "told"—truly or not is beyond my comprehension—that these were the names of women who had been murdered, then dropped into a well on the grounds. More, the Captain believed the murderer to be his own son. Finally—or so the séances were to intimate—the son had killed the father.

All these revelations—and the rest, incredibly to follow—would not occur until after the couple, for understandable reasons, left the old home for their own apartment. In moved a young Vietnam Navy veteran who, through an unnerving two weeks immediately awaiting him, would become a friend of Neal's—an intimacy born of facing the unknown.

The new tenant seemed no more than a powerfully-built and much decorated veteran of Mekong Delta gunboat fighting. Here, he settled into gracious lodgings where he hoped to forget things.

At three in the morning, early into his residence, the phone waked him. A relative was hospitalized—an auto wreck. No hour for visiting, he sleepily told himself and turned back to his pillow. Below him, he felt the mattress jerk angrily.

"Get up!" a voice commanded from the dark. "Get out of here!"

Dreams, he thought, and again sought sleep. Violently, something hurled his mattress upwards, its sleeper slamming into the wall. And then the room went black. So he left and made the hospital visit. In the morning he called Neal—what was wrong with that house?

By degrees, what Kitty had kept from her husband began to come out. He was horrified.

Again, Neal's new tenant called. Someone was dragging heavy things about the attic above him, always at three in the morning. At first he defied it, returning to sleep. But it waked him again, louder than before. Each time he tried to sleep, the noise would wake him within an hour. Eventually he would force himself awake and try to face the morning, early though it was. But then the clock would rewind itself, showing the time to still only be three o'clock.

"What the hell's wrong with this house . . . what's in the attic?" he asked Neal. Together, they determined to summon psychic help. The first medium confessed knowledge of little beyond the Ouija Board; shortly, a parapsychologist would join, and the reporter, Dick Bryant. A group confronted that room, and the séances began.

The Ouija—considered by some an extension of automatic writing, and by others, a dangerous plaything—dominated these sessions. It gave confusing answers.

The killer, it suggested, was a madman. His victims: two girls with names like Kitty's. The father sought to protect her. Yet, he was a victim too. Which of them was maneuvering the Ouija? Why was the Navy man attacked? Perhaps he resembled the hated son.

At some point, the young veteran recalled another manifestation: even while telephoning Neal, he had seen a picture plucked from the desk and floated across to lodge before his startled eyes. There was a picture in the attic, Ouija observed.

They went to the attic and found the picture: some resemblance could be seen, and the Navy veteran was shaken. In Vietnam, a man could see to shoot back; this was different. All this, reporter Dick Bryant recorded with care. However, in the end, his exhaustive investigation showed that Colonel Marcus Mott, builder of the house, had been a nothing but a highly respected Galveston citizen. It made no sense.

Yet here was Ouija insisting that Mott kin—unknown to anyone—could be found in Colorado, a fact confirmed later. The sessions dragged on, night after night. Finally the parapsychologist took Neal and Kitty aside, telling them they should stop the sessions. This spirit—whoever it was—was dangerous.

But perhaps it was too late. Perhaps they had started something that could not be stopped. The Navy veteran became increasingly tense, and as a result he called Neal more and more frequently. They were directed to a book in the attic, opened as though by design: there was a reference to an important trunk. What trunk? The attic was a jumble of things long forgotten. They found no trunk. At first.

And then a voice again woke the veteran at three a.m. It was a woman's voice, seductive, calling his name. She was just outside the door.

But when he opened the door, the hallway was dark and empty. From the attic stairway, from its top, the voice echoed in the dark space. He climbed. The voice was inside. He drew a deep breath . . . and went in.

This was a powerful young man who worked out with weights. Yet in the enveloping gloom, something seemed to smother that strength, encircling him, wrapping itself round and round. Like Kitty's stifling lethargy on the bed, he felt unable to move, as though bound to one of the big supporting attic pillars.

He struggled to free himself. In the morning, Neal Witwer found an agitated man whose wrists bore rope burns, whose ribs seemed bruised.

No one longer doubted that some being had guided the Ouija: for a long period it had fallen silent, then suddenly resumed. The spirit had rested, it explained. In the adjoining bedroom, fresh bedclothes were now rumpled. The woman who'd spoken to the veteran was one of the victims of the son.

The attic trunk seemed forgotten; the Ouija psychic was speaking now of something to occur at midnight—which midnight, she was unsure. It disturbed her. So the séances were stopped—what had they revealed beyond the presence of danger in the Mott House?

That night, Neal and his wife remained in their apartment, the husband grateful for a quiet evening. Then Kitty burst into the room.

"Call the house!" she cried out. "Tell him to get that trunk out of the room!"

Neil looked at her, astonished, then reached for the telephone.

"Good God!" came his Navy friend's answer. "We just brought a steamer trunk down from the attic. It's right beside me now!" There was a long silence.   Then the vet explained that he was getting out of there, going to stay at a friend's.

Neal, both impulsive and methodical, glanced at the clock: not yet midnight. He waited. As the hour struck, he heard his wife. In nightdress, she was hurriedly preparing to leave.

"I've got to go to the house!" she insisted. It didn't seem to matter how she was dressed.

She had to be in some kind of trance. Forcibly, he restrained her. In the morning he called the apartment where his Navy friend had moved in. Exactly on Ouija's hour, that man had fought off the compulsion that drew them back to the formidable gray dwelling.

Shortly, the veteran left Galveston. Shortly, too, Neal Witwer faced divorce and Kitty left the city. The house was too much for her, he supposed. So far as he knew, she was happily married now. He certainly was.

"Nothing in these quarters bothers *this* marriage," he told me. "Everything's quiet once more."

"What about your Navy friend?" I asked. "Should I talk with him?"

"He's in North Texas, married . . . I'd leave him alone. You couldn't get him inside this house again." Neal paused. "Why even remind him of it?"

"And the trunk?" I asked. "The one he brought down?"

"I don't know," he said honestly. "Maybe it was hauled away . . ." His voice trailed off, he did not say by whom.

"What about the thing in the attic?"

It's quiet, Neal said. Those who brought back recollections, I suppose you could argue, are all gone now. Over a century's time, so many dwellers knew that place. So much could have happened.

And the bodies it suggested? A well has never been found on the property.

The attic itself? When I climbed up there, I made no effort to pry into anything. Why disturb what a century's dust prefers concealed? I left the Mott House with the briefest backward glance. Tall and stern, its gabled attic was the last thing I saw.

Perhaps something watched me leave.

EDITOR'S NOTE: While this story was widely reported in the media at the time, there are variations. One version states that it was the arrival of the boarder that caused the ghost to initially become active; also, that the Witwers lived there at the same time as the tenant in separate rooms.

Both Neal's wife and their tenant have been named in other accounts of this tale. Out of respect for Ed's decision to protect their identities, the names remain changed in this account.

THE RACER

San Diego, Freer, Duval County

I walked into the formidable old brick courthouse in San Diego to ask directions to a place the past knew well. "I suppose it's on private land," I said to a lean man in jeans and a Stetson. This was Johnny Webb, a lifetime resident who has drilled for oil or gas across much of his county. He knew the place—west, toward Freer.

"Yeah," he said after detailing the way, "it's private, all right. But, mister, every inch of this country is private land."

After that, he and his wife Cristela, who handles Duval unemployment for the state commission, unfolded part of the story I sought.

"It's not much more than a cattle tank now," Johnny Webb said. "A creek runs in and then out." He looked at me appraisingly. "People don't like to be around there. Funny things happen."

"They see lights where there aren't any," his wife added. "Strange sounds and . . ." Her voice trailed off; she did not want to consider the grimly purposeful horseman still riding that brush on dark nights.

San Diego, seat of rule in the stern land that is Duval County, is a listless and sagging place known in the recent past mainly to office seekers in pursuit of bloc votes. It is difficult to imagine this rolling thatch of mesquite and sage as once centering prosperous ranch country.

In the late 1800s, prospering ranchers knew the little lake and its thin fringe of trees. It had always promised a good campsite in land where water was scarce, but by the mid-1800s it bore a name to avoid, and a deadly reason for that name.

All this, however, was unknown to a couple wagoning across the rough country early in the 1900s. These intended to visit a kinsman near San Diego, but dark was overtaking them. Across the distant brush the man saw the faint flicker of campfire, and he made for it. With hard dark, they came on the little lake.

There was no fire, nor trace of ashes. Could he have imagined it? Beside the lake, glinting leaden in a thin wood, he struck a sulfur match and contrived his own firelight. Wood and water—a good campsite. He turned to help his wife unload their wagon. She stood motionless, listening.

He, too, heard the hoofbeats, drumming louder, coming fast. Instinctively he kicked out his fire, and put a protective arm around his wife's shoulders. Only a crazy man would race a horse through that black tangle of brush. Such a man could be dangerous.

The horseman burst from the night, up on a gaunt gray stallion, unnaturally visible in this gloom. But on the instant of visibility, the hammer of hooves snuffed out, and in dead silence, the thing was on them.

"*Madre de dios!*" The woman gasped and fainted.

Bending to drive his mount to its limit, the rider had no head.

He blew by, soundless, straight to the mirror lake. Yet not into it . . . on top, a gray flash across the dead-still surface. At the far tree line, horseman and mount vanished.

With frantic haste, the man revived his wife, broke camp, and whipped his team out of there.

Juan Sauvageau, linguistics professor at Texas A&M University in Kingsville, has preserved many rich South Texas legends in his three-volume *Tales That Must Not Die* (PSI Research, 1985), an intriguing bilingual work. Sauvageau found the story behind that phantom horseman.

Early ranchers of this lonely land found horse-racing their favorite respite from monotony. This lakeside provided a straightaway for their matched contests.

In all that broad country, four horses were judged fastest; inevitably they were pitted against each other, a climactic occasion. Before the race, the owners—friends all—began such an event with a good-natured drinking bout. While drinking, they bet.

Much too long, they drank; far too much, they bet. The owner of the big gray bet with condescending arrogance. Goaded, the others bet all they owned.

But when the big gray won that race, fury burst. Nothing could run that fast—he must have doctored that horse! Who went first for his gun is not known, but it is known that the gray's owner fell.

It was not enough—not for their humiliation. With a machete, they beheaded him, then buried him in the near brush. From a distance, the gray stallion saw it and ran, never again to be caught; its range was too broad, broken and empty.

Those men would see the stallion again, as would others, but only when night came to this lake where the race was run . . . such a night as the fleeing couple had experienced.

On a later morning, the story goes, the man returned with his wife and kinsmen. No sign remained of the camp they had made, the wagon ruts, the fire he had kicked out. Nowhere in the lakeside mud was the mark of a single hoof.

"But it happened!" the man protested.

"The ranchero rides for all to see," the kinsman said. "He's proving that his stallion won the race fairly."

Time and lack of rain have shrunk the lake, the Johnny Webbs pointed out, so much that one would pass by without a second glance. I would find it best by daylight; and, of course, I must seek permission. After all, the land *is* privately occupied.

"Do you know what we call the place?" Cristela Webb asked me. "Do you know what 'La Muralla' means?"

"I've heard the place called 'Dead Man's Lake.'"

It meant a little more than that, she said.

For a while afterward, I asked around San Diego—what was known of the headless rider. I received an occasional shrug or smile. How could one, obviously not of this land, understand? Of one aged man in a little shop on the edge of town, I asked—without preamble—what had happened to the other three who killed the ranchero.

He made a slight, silent gesture. Death comes for all men.

And so, the following morning I passed the lake and its time-erased racing course, some eleven miles west of San Diego where the land is rolling mesquite and huisache, dappled in cenzio and lanced with cactus. It lies northward in the direction of the tall palms and the home atop a distant small hill.

You would be advised to view it from there, too. Look about you. Beside the lake, the terrain is the same.

And it *is* privately owned, both by day . . . and by night.

EDITOR'S NOTE: Many folklorists link this story to the one of Creed Taylor and Bigfoot Wallace that was recounted earlier in the book. Some say this headless horseman is in fact Vidal, El Muerto himself. There are only sixteen miles between Ben Bolt, where Vidal was buried, and San Diego. A ghostly rider could probably traverse that distance.

The sightings of the rider in San Diego continue to this day. The now completely dry lake is still avoided at night, and still privately owned.

Juan Sauvagneau's *Stories That Must Not Die* is still available and highly recommended. Many of the individual stories were republished in small editions by National Education Services in 2012, with illustrations by Xavier Garza.

LIENDO

Hempstead, Brazos

The gasping cry waked the man. He knew it was the child, out there in the vast dark that enveloped the oaks and river meadows of the plantation.

He did not want to look. He knew who the child was.

Beyond that window toward the cemetery, it would be watching, calling for help. But finally the sound of distress was too much. He had to look. And it was there. Small and feeble at the line of trees. Watching.

In the morning the man quit his job. An ordinary cowboy was not supposed to handle the inexplicable.

He didn't explain. How do you tell someone that you lie awake at night, terrified at the sound of a small child's cry?

How do you pick up a coffee cup and explain what you've just seen? How do you admit that the fear comes from seeing through the unopened door, the tilted glimpse into the void beyond? How do you explain the unexplainable?

You don't, the man had decided. Everyone was tolerant of the brief excuses he gave, even in town. Of course, they knew; they just didn't talk about it.

This man, who wishes to remain anonymous, shows how hard it was to secure help from town for the 1,100-acre Plantation Liendo Ranch, historic and magnificent in its rolling live oak forest near Hempstead, close by the coastal Brazos. How can a man identify himself when everyone knows that ghosts are visions of the simple and the superstitious? Plantation foreman Dick Gannaway, a strong-faced, practical man, shrugs away what night may bring. He admits that others who have spent the night in Liendo's guest bunkhouse believe they have experienced a visitant. He and his wife know Liendo's story, one of this state's most unusual.

To understand it, you turn back the years, for the splendidly restored white two-story and its forested bottomlands are old in our history.

The land was originally farmed in 1833—eleven leagues of it then—by Jose Justo Liendo, who possessed an original Spanish grant. From him, it was bought by Colonel Leonard Groce in 1849. Near here, Groce's father had sustained Sam Houston's ragged army just before the march for San Jacinto.

The big home went up in 1853—Georgia longleaf pine freighted in from Houston, marble mantels, six fireplaces beyond its columned façade. Slave-built brick made its foundations and outbuildings. In its day it provided lavish hospitality for early Texas and knew every formidable name in this territory.

But Civil War broke Colonel Groce, and Liendo changed hands. Immediately after the war, it briefly served as a headquarters for General George Armstrong Custer.

Its most extraordinary occupants arrived in the early 1870s—famed German sculptor Elisabet Ney and her partner, the equally distinguished Dr. Edmund Montgomery. He was a Scotsman who delved into biology and philosophy.

Europe's world of art and science had claimed both, but their version of coupled life was out of tune with their time. The fiery woman who had sculpted kings and the head-strong doctor both disavowed marriage—Montgomery wasn't her husband. They were best friends. He addressed her as "Miss Ney."

She bedecked herself in a Roman toga and a turban. As had been their experience in Georgia, where they first settled, this lifestyle of theirs was too much for unreconstructed Hempstead; nearby Texans viewed the couple with open scorn.

Hermitlike, with near-primitive furnishings, the two tried to make a go of Liendo Plantation, but ultimately failed—altogether another story. Elisabet finally left for Austin—the state capitol houses her heroic Texas works—and died there in 1907 at age seventy-four. Montgomery would live out his life in Liendo. Both are buried in the little cemetery plot below the restored home they once occupied.

So is their son Arthur who, story holds, is the child who calls for help across the dark nights.

A defiant individualist, Elisabet had dressed their younger son, Lorne, in the Roman garb that she also wore. That this further alienated the family from the people of Hempstead and made for one son's unhappy life soon became of minor importance to the mother. Her eldest, Arthur, soon dominated all her concern.

A diphtheria epidemic was sweeping the South Texas woodlands, and the child was close to death. The parents fought for their son's life, and lost.

To block contagion, Elisabet first barred Liendo from all visitation. When the boy died, she and Montgomery chose the living room fireplace as a crematorium for Arthur. There, grief-stricken, they burned the child's body.

For a time, the ashes were kept in an urn on the mantel. Eventually, the urn would join both parents in the small plot behind the great house.

Chuck McCollough, who published the *Waller County News Citizen*, has said that no one is sure when the hauntings began. After Elisabet's flight from the home, most of the staff also left. The house aged and sagged, and Hempstead citizens knew it to be inhabited by phantoms. A succession of owners followed until 1960, when Carl and Phylis Detering bought it.

Over the next decade Liendo was painstakingly restored. It became a jewel-like reminder of forgotten times. It is also a home that can be viewed only by appointment. The Hempstead publisher took me out. If Liendo's owners are quite obviously untroubled by specters, foreman Dick Gannaway admits that help is hard to come by because of them. He may smile at the plantation's visitants, but he acknowledges that others have sensed them.

The long white guesthouse, well apart from the home, is where—come hard dark—the child may return. Many who have spent the night there believe they have heard the tiny, gasping cry. And, like the cowboy who rode herd so briefly, those of Liendo understandably prefer not to discuss it.

Yet there are some still in Hempstead who have grown up knowing that the child comes crying in the night. Do his parents not also arise to help?

Apparently the restorers of Liendo ignore such tales. Theirs is a beautifully secluded home away from the hectic pace of Houston. And just as they are aware that they reinstated an early Texas showplace, they also value privacy, which a home should provide.

Some four miles northeast of Hempstead, off Whiting Chapel Road, it slumbers behind its rolling wall of timber. The day I visited the grounds followed a weekend of filming by a network television crew—the house providing a setting for a new series. Had the ghosts bothered anyone?

No one would say either way. Liendo was far more concerned with the gate, which someone—it had to be that TV crew—had left open. Valuable Brahman cattle had wandered out on the road all night.

As I drove away into a summer morning, the opened gate traveled with me. Was it really the television crew who left it, swung wide? Or could it have been others, disturbed by too many people?

EDITOR'S NOTE: Today, Liendo is owned by Carl and Phylis Detering's son, Will. It is now a cultural landmark and living museum that is open once a month for tours and weddings. They also host a very popular Civil War reenactment.

WILL'S HOUSE

Dallas–Forth Worth Area

This is my house!" The young woman's voice hardened. "Mine. Get out of my house!" The young woman's tones had become masculine, threatening.

The attending psychic was leaning forward, absorbing every hypnotized word, as was her tape recorder. It was then that she saw the woman's hands rising from rest on the tabletop, reaching slowly for her throat. The psychic held out the cross she had brought, cut the recorder, and broke the trance. It was unsafe to go on.

This spirit was hostile to the point of danger. The other two voices, those that also had taken over the woman's speech while she was in the trance, were friendly, protective. But in this house, the man was dominant. The psychic feared him.

So, she advised, should Jean—the name we will give to this young woman who had been hypnotized. Shortly thereafter, in November 1979, Jean's husband moved her and their daughter to an apartment in one of the satellite cities of the Dallas–Fort Worth area. Jean sent me the psychic's tape and, while visiting with her, I learned as much of the story as is available to us.

We drove to the house, comfortably handsome brick in a quiet neighborhood. Since Jean left, three families had come and gone. The house was vacant again.

Unoccupied? Jean would say not. And this pretty young outdoors-woman—she grew up riding a West Texas ranch—is as difficult to label superstitious as are the computers she operates these days.

However, she has reached frightened certainty on the house that drove her and her family out. Within it dwell at least three spirits. One is that of the man whom many call Will. The others are a mother and her small son.

Walking about the place, apparently untended in the latter days of its last occupancy and obviously abandoned in haste, I tried to picture the home, which Jean first entered in happiness. Three bedrooms, two baths, and a nice lawn: you've seen hundreds like it.

"The very first day," she recalled, "I felt something wrong: a heavi-ness, a sadness . . . I told my husband I could feel hostility, as though something didn't want us there. He said I was just tired from moving."

Still, the uneasiness grew. How could a practical woman, Jean asked herself, feel that someone else was very close, watching her? There were no such things as ghosts.

"Then one night, a week or two later," she said, "my husband had taken our daughter to a shopping mall. I was in the living room, here by the glass doors. So was someone else—I was sure of it.

"Before I knew it, I said out loud that if someone was really there, they should let me know, show me some kind of sign."

A voice "spoke to her mind." She was not prepared to see them, not yet. Let her instead watch the big hanging basket and the chandelier.

Jean directed her gaze to the heavy pieces; moving them would take force. Yet before her eyes they were swinging in great arcs. In puzzled recollection, she shook her head. "That moment, my husband drove up. The swinging didn't slow down. It stopped instantly."

A longtime neighborhood resident came visiting, welcoming the new family to the area. Jean asked her if anything unusual had ever hap-pened here. The woman turned pale, then, little by little, told what she had observed over the dwelling's lifespan.

A few years earlier, a man she believed to be named Will had built this home, intending to make it his own. He seemed a good man, an asset to the neighborhood; then financial difficulties beset him. Perhaps the house had overextended him. He lost it and not long after died suddenly—a bitter, angry man, the neighbor believed.

"I think he determined that he would occupy this house," she told Jean, "no matter who tried to move in." Hadn't Jean felt a terrible hostility? Everyone else had.

The house then changed hands rapidly. Through the nights, the television, the radio, the lights turned on and off. Doors and windows opened and closed; there were inexplicable noises—all the neighborhood knew it, this neighbor more than any, because she always visited newcomers, even though they came and went so quickly . . . and were always deeply troubled.

To this neighbor, it was as though some force changed the very character of those who came here to live. In happy families, bitterness set in; differences flared; separations threatened. Children spoke of visitors no one else had seen; they became ill without cause or outward symptoms.

Over these short years, nine families had come and gone, most within three months. Will, the neighbor believed, possessed someone in each family and, that way, drove all of them out. In a way, he failed once, for part of one family remained.

After a violent argument, a husband had walked out, finished with marriage. The distraught wife, her small son beside her, wrecked her car leaving the house in a hurry. They both died instantly.

"She was a sweet, lovely lady," the neighbor told Jean. "I think that she and her son are here, too . . . in their way, resisting Will's influence."

The other voices on her tapes. A woman, and a boy.

"We've seen what must have been the boy's form, his shadow . . . whatever. And then our daughter began to 'talk' with him . . ." Jean paused, frowning. "Then it occurred to me why the mother wouldn't show herself that night—the way she must have looked, after the accident."

"Will never showed himself?" I asked.

"Only in the possession of others," she said. "At least that's what the psychic and my neighbor believed. I guess, finally, so did I: my husband and I began to fight over nothing at all."

As fear of the house grew, she called her mother, who brought over the psychic. It didn't help: Jean couldn't believe what she heard on the tape. "All my husband said," she reflected, "was that it wasn't my voice. He agreed it was time to move."

Afterward, though she feared to go near the place, there remained a frightening fascination about it; she kept up through her former neighbor. "Following us, there was a woman with two big Dobermans. The dogs didn't want to go inside but, to protect her, they would—right on her heels, as though something was about to happen. Then one night, one of the dogs died in the backyard, and the veterinarian could find no cause. The woman moved, too."

One following occupant became a good friend of Jean's former neighbor; yet she, too, was to undergo extraordinary change, living in that house. The two friends had planned a shopping trip, and, when it was time, Jean's neighbor went down to see when the other would be ready. The woman's dog, always friendly, attacked her. Then, the lady came to the door, looked her in the eye and said, "Get out of my house!"

"Will," I broke in. "Just as on your tape."

The house had only been abandoned the day before I had driven up from Kerrville. The tenants had left in what appeared extreme haste, some of their belongings scattered on the floor.

"A mighty big hurry to leave," I said.

Jean gestured in frustration. "Since you were coming, I got up enough courage to come ask them to speak to you, and I found them leaving. I asked if anything had happened, and they looked badly frightened." She paused. "They promised to talk with you. I guess they ran instead."

Back at Jean's apartment, we talked of her family and the tranquility of their present quarters. Still it was hard to get away from the place we had just left.

I wondered if Will would ever show himself.

Probably not the way I meant it, Jean thought. Possession—of the house and of those within it—was his way of terrifying.

She reflected for a moment. Was it possible, also, that he wanted to avoid recognition? The psychic believed that Will was not the man who built the house and then lost it. She saw a dangerous being that let the builder finish the place, then took it from him.

Could that mean that the builder himself had fallen victim? Jean didn't know.

Finally I left. Speculation was solving nothing and Jean was trying to move beyond her experience.

Perhaps all that matters is that I not reveal the address. Besides, as has already been stated, the address is not important. What's important is the fact that this house belongs to Will.

THE WHITE SEÑORITA

Laredo

As America's major gateway to Mexico, Laredo presents a procession of Latin-flavored buildings arrayed along a broad expressway that reaches to the handsome international bridge.

However, east and west of that bridge—the Rio Grande makes a giant southward loop—the old town stretches out, shoulder-to-shoulder dwellings with tucked-away patios crowding close on narrow streets. It is in old Laredo that you may learn of the White Señorita.

The old ones know her story, and although much has changed in the city that she graced long ago, she is still there, close by the river. On certain dark nights she may be seen. You will recognize her—the beautifully sad face, the raven hair, the flowing white gown.

Of course, this lovely girl is dead, but she has a purpose. As those with ancient wisdom can tell you, given purpose of sufficient strength, the dead can return.

Some years ago, the White Señorita's story was related to the folklorist Henry Yelvington by a Laredo woman, long in residence near the great bend of the river. I talked with Luciano Guajardo, who directed Laredo's fine library and who knew his city as do very few.

The girl was Juanita Sepulveda, and Luciano—tall and graying with intense eyes—smiles approvingly when he considers her. You have no doubt that this amiable and articulate historian could show you where she stands watch.

In the early days, tiny Laredo crowded about what is now shaded San Agustín Plaza, and its outlying brasada, the rolling homeland of great ranchos. On one of them, the large family of Juan Sepulveda prospered happily. There were lean, strong sons and, pride of that family, the lissome girl with dark hair and eyes, and skin like cream—Juanita.

Pride of the Sepulvedas, yes . . . yet a source of nagging concern, and that was felt most keenly by her eldest brother, Pedro. There was a brash young man who came dressed like a true *rico*, calling himself a ranchero from interior Mexico. Miguel Cervantes, he called himself, and boldly he let his interest in Juanita be seen.

It was not enough that the girl already had promised her hand to the Sepulveda's good friend and neighbor, Antonio de la Garza. She openly flirted with this Miguel. Her brother suspected that the man was a bandit, the herds he boasted, stolen.

In that still empty country, cross-river cattle raids were common. The man disappeared into Mexico too frequently. He was too vague as to the site of his hacienda. And there were those who believed they had seen him riding the night with dangerous men.

Yet there he was, all smiles and grace, promenading the plaza with Juanita!

As a reliable son should, Pedro went to his father. The Sepulveda herds— many carried their brand—were in danger. Then the son drew a breath of decision and spoke of the man's attentions to Juanita.

The father's decree was instant: Miguel Cervantes was no longer welcome at Hacienda Sepulveda. Juanita was forbidden even to glance at him.

And so it was that her brother could relax a little, even enough to ride for Monterrey's Cinco de Mayo Fiesta, even enough to take with him two kinsmen and Juanita's husband-to-be. A proper bachelor celebration before the bonds of marriage—why not?

Yet in the very midst of Monterrey gaiety, the brother felt unaccount-ably mounting anxiety, and finally the outright premonition that only immediate family can sense for one of its own. They must ride back to Laredo! Protesting, the companions rode nonetheless, and Pedro pushed them unrelentingly. With twilight of the third day, they reined up in the chaparral along Rio Bravo.

Pedro had motioned them to silence. Faintly they could hear dis-tant hoofbeats. Into the thickest brush they rode and waited until there within earshot, Miguel Cervantes—no ranchero but outright bandito—sat his saddle with four riders. Revelation came quickly.

When the others—pistoleros handpicked by Miguel—joined, all of them would strike the Sepulveda rancho. Every cow! And the girl, too! Oh, she had seen him secretly, true enough; but now she refused to ride away with him. Well, they would take her . . . and this very night!

With a furious shout, the Sepulvedas charged, husband-to-be Antonio in the lead; savage, close-quarter fire stabbed the darkness. Then it was over, two pistoleros down, the others fleeing, their leader hit and sway-ing in the saddle. The arm of Juanita's brother was shattered, but dead on the ground was the man she was pledged to marry.

They carried Antonio to the rancho. Let the girl see what coquetry had brought upon them!

This, perhaps, they should not have done. That night, Juanita, robed in wedding white, came alone from the great house. In the morning they found her in the garden, a cameo portrait of Antonio pressed against her heart.

For a moment with me, these long years after, Luciano Guajardo pondered the intensity of emotion that beset the girl, those last mo-ments of her life. Guilt and shame. The engulfment of tragedy she had caused! How to do penance?

With one of such quality, the old and wise of Laredo know, death was not enough to pay for what she had done. By nights they began to see her close by the river. Some thought they recognized her—haunting beauty glimpsed momentarily.

Others knew what they faced when, fearing intruders in disguise, they fired at close range. For the true White Señorita, such bullets were harmless.

The certainty of Juanita's identity and, more important, the purpose for her returning, came about only gradually. She materialized with no regularity. Usually, however, the night was very dark—such a night as that which Cervantes, the bandito, had chosen to cross Rio Bravo.

An aged watchman, of whom searcher Henry Yelvington had learned, disclosed what those along the Bravo had long known but rarely discussed. This watchman, in the darkest of night, had come face-to-face with an apparition in white and had fired three shots point blank. Always the chance of a bad man in disguise, he would later explain.

The bullets did no harm: it was the lovely Juanita, and she had come—as always—to warn of impending danger, crossing the river that very night.

And that night, Yelvington would learn, two smugglers, long wanted on both sides of the Rio Grande, has been shot dead on its banks.

That discovery in no way surprised Luciano Guajardo. He is acquainted with those of Laredo who are knowledgeable of such matters.

Of course, the White Señorita comes back on certain gloomy nights, the kind of darkness chosen to cover those who would cross Rio Bravo with evil intent. What else would one expect from a lovely girl always true in her heart? What other way would she choose to do proper penance?

And in really old Laredo, there are those—if they trust you—who could show you where she walks her vigil. If you are patient enough, they very likely could show her to you.

Does my friend Luciano Guajardo know this to be fact? He smiles and shrugs.

"Bad men still cross the river," he observes. "From both sides."

THE JUG HUNTER

Bailey's Prairie, Brazoria Country, Brazosport

Hard dark came wet and black across the prairie, a misting late fall night that was bleak for this coastal country where the Brazos slipped through moss-draped oaks and stole out to sea.

Even twilight had settled gloomily. The woman observed that she could scarcely see the nearby pecan grove. At a mile away, the dim lamps of their nearest neighbor were unseen.

The blackness was such that she could barely detect the night sky through the little window of her room. Darkness had never really frightened her, nor had this house, for when her husband had bought it, no one had told her its story. Besides, only a brave woman would make a home in the wilderness that was the new Republic of Texas in the autumn of 1836.

Still, she had slept restlessly. And now, deep within the small, still hours, she was awake. Something had wakened her and, more than that, it was within her room. She could not see the servant girl's cot beside the opposite wall. But she could feel another presence.

Something that was unnaturally cold, colder than night air, had come in.

Slowly she shifted her gaze to the door.

Indistinct, there was a form—a man's form, big, opaque as though not altogether solid. With the shuddering prescience given to those who face such encounters, she knew the man was dead. He did not seem to advance, but only to loom. She tried to cry out, but her voice froze.

Quickly he was standing over her bed, as formless and faceless as he had been by the door. He was bending over her. She tried to shut her eyes but could not. He had to know that her eyes, wide in terror, were fixed on him. She could not move.

But it was not for her that he was reaching. He began groping beneath the bed. Not finding what he was after, the figure retreated to the door, and then into invisibility.

In the morning, the servant girl told Ann Thomas that she was sleeping in the very bed where the man had died four years earlier. Yes, the girl had seen everything. She had been too terrified to make a sound.

Ann's husband, John Thomas, back from a brief trip, told his wife that she had experienced a nightmare. To think nothing of it.

Certainly he had known all the tales when he'd bought the red house on Bennett's Ridge. The haunting, he chuckled, had made its purchase easier. And, of course, he would sleep in the room if it disturbed her. Brit Bailey—that's who he thought she saw—had been his friend; he might just up and shake the old man's hand.

He never did. In the opposite bedroom nights later, Ann waked to a scream hoarse with terror. This time, she could move. She burst into the room, and on the edge of the bed, the sweat beading on his face, her husband sat rigid, staring at something beyond her sight.

"It was old man Bailey," her husband finally gasped. "I saw him plain as day!"

That was more than a century and a half ago. But above coastal Brazosport, where the river separates East and West Columbia, those who know Bailey's Prairie know that the old man has never given up returning to the land that was his. A roadside marker admits this.

Catherine Munson Foster of Angleton, a fifth-generation Brazorian, knows Bailey's Prairie perhaps better than any. She knows that Brit comes back to search for something. If his will had been carried out as directed, perhaps he never would have returned at all.

One of Texas's earliest Anglo settlers, North Carolinian James Britton Bailey, settled his family on Bennett's Ridge in 1818 on the highest elevation in that moss-decked coastal forest.

Old Brit—that was how he came to be known—was a big man, exceptional in a country that could be tamed only by extraordinary men. He was a man of integrity, and fearless, folks agreed, but there were also certain things—eccentricities—about him. For one thing, he liked to fight. For another—even more than he liked to fight—he was a devotee of the jug, always close by.

In his stark red house, some five miles east of the Brazos, Brit's eccentricities grew to prodigal proportions. Boot-shooting—to encourage a man's dancing—was one example.

When Old Brit died of "the fever" in December of 1832, he left a will that really should have surprised no one. It was his supreme gesture.

Bury him erect—he had never bowed to any man. Face him west— he always aimed in that direction. Place his rifle by his side—who knew what enemies awaited a man in the great beyond?

And at his feet, leave his jug, full to the cork.

Confronting the preacher, his wife managed each stipulation one at a time. Then she got to the jug . . . and there stood Brit's favorite retainer, ready to lower away. But also, there stood the preacher. And that was when she broke Brit Bailey's will, refusing to place the jug in the coffin.

Presently the gaunt house was sold. For the Bailey family, too many memories. For others, a different matter: the old man knew that his will—and it was an iron one—had not been obeyed. And Brit Bailey wasn't one to give up.

As the years turned—the Thomases had moved, of course—the old house began to decay. Across Bailey's Prairie, however, there was whispered talk. Something luminescent moved about through those trees near Brit's grave.

In the 1850s, Colonel Mordello Munson, Catherine Foster's forebear, was wakened by the frightened cries of his hounds. Out he went. A great column of fiery light, the size of a big man, stood in the yard. Through much of that night Colonel Munson pursued it on horseback. Each time he neared, it vanished only to reappear at some considerable distance.

Regularly in those days, others saw it, almost always on a late fall or early winter night. Something was abroad out there, something that could unlock gates, climb fences, or pass through them. Always it circled as though in absorbed search.

Gradually the visitations lessened, as did the size of the specter. Perhaps even Brit's iron determination could not sustain an apparition for so long a time. Those who know about such things recognized that he was resisting the inevitable passing over. Now his light was the size of a barrel, then no more than that of a churn, and, more recently, the size of a lantern. Yet always, there was that fiery intensity at its center.

Around old Columbia, some claim that Brit can make it back only every seven years—a kind of hoarding-up of sufficient strength. In 1939 he startled a driver off the road. In '46 and again in '53 and '60, his light, progressively smaller as might be expected, was nonetheless still seen wandering his prairie.

They say he has stopped cars dead on the road, has toyed with various mechanisms—surely strange to him—such as windshield wipers. Some claim he even caused a gas blowout when drillers worked too close to his grave—a site somewhere along the slight ridge.

Of course, if you accept the seven-year timetable, Brit should have shown himself sometime in 1981.

There are those, naturally, who know that the chill of autumn makes for times best suited to warm a man's insides with a good pull from the jug. Doubtless a two-fisted drinker may see the searcher before we, the normally curious, do.

And then there are those—perhaps even you—who disbelieve that Old Brit comes back at all. Fireballs, foxfire . . . that sort of thing. Finally, there are certain optimists who are sure that the search has ended. Back in 1836, Brit Bailey meant no harm—you have, of course, recognized this by now—to the lady in his bed. He wanted his jug. And wherever his wife hid it, maybe he's finally found it.

EDITOR'S NOTE: Using Ed's math and the seven-year schedule, Brit should make an appearance sometime in the fall of 2016, and then again in 2023.

WOLF WOMAN

Devil's River, Del Rio, Brackettville

Beyond San Felipe Springs, before westward Del Rio grew up along its lush banks, the California Road veered north up the Devil's River Canyon, a thin and remote trail. Walled by close bluffs, it climbed a land of weirs, spires and brooding rock.

In the mid-1800s, this was the best way to the new, western gold fields; and, creaking along the emptiness, the emigrant wagons came by ones, twos, and long trains. Above the whisper of its water, the canyon stillness echoed to their labored coming. Here, point riders watched the heights: this was ambush country.

The lone rider knew this. He was up ahead of the single wagon that carried his family and, intently, he studied the high rock, chill in autumn twilight. It was not Comanche he feared—rather, something he could not believe he really had seen. Camp Hudson, the solitary mid-canyon outpost, was just ahead. He drove for it.

As night came on, he led his wagon into the little post, found quarters for his family, and made for the saloon. After the second whiskey, he spoke with careful offhandedness. Along the road behind, he thought he had seen something strange.

"It was hairy all over—looked like a big wolf." He poured another whiskey, his eyes remaining fixed on it. "It had a face like you and me."

Down the bar, a sergeant looked up. He knew about the wolf woman.

Like other educated men who, for whatever disillusionment, lost themselves west, the sergeant drank too much. Sometimes it was hard to recall
all that he had read in a happier time. Herodotus and Virgil, he could remember—those ancient scholars who tried to explain how, under certain
conditions, man could turn into wolf. Reading further, he had learned that,
from the drear Balkan forests to the Scottish moors and to Africa, wolf men
were believed to be realities.

He had forgotten all that until, out here, he heard of that English
colony southeast of them along the Rio Grande. Some twenty years earlier it had been virtually annihilated . . . and there was talk of a baby girl
taken by wolves. He wasn't sure of the whole story.

But he was sure about the wagon train, through last month, and
about last week's westbound stage.

Both had seen the wolf woman.

Now, not much is known of the John Charles Beales colony of Dolores,
lost in the stormy months that began the Texas Revolution. It had been
part of Mexico's latest and largest land grant, an empire reaching from
the Nueces out beyond Paso del Norte. Beales was English; so were most
of his colonists, the last of whom settled in 1834, just below the present-
day site of Brackettville.

From the beginning, Dolores's struggle against drought and nearby
Natives was a losing one. Its collapse was complete when Santa Anna
marched north. The last handful of settlers, fleeing ahead, was wiped
out by Comanche along the old Presidio Road. Only two women survived for later ransom.

History is noncommittal about a third woman, Mollie Pertul Dent,
who had followed her husband, John, up the Devil's River to a camp at
Beaver Lake, just north of Camp Hudson. Dent contrived shelter and
found a rich run of beaver—so rewarding that fall had crept into winter
before the Englishman realized the trees were bare.

Unaware of the Dolores disaster, John Dent toiled on, believing
they would have money if he could win his race against time. Soon he
must take his wife the long way back to a doctor in San Antonio—she

carried their child. She could wait a little longer, she had told him, and they needed the money.

But they waited too long. There was no mistaking the birth pains. For one horrified instant Dent felt the trap of their isolation. San Antonio was too far. So was Dolores. Off to the west, Mexican sheepherders grazed the Pecos Valley. Maybe their women would help?

And so, out of a terrible night thunderstorm, the shepherds saw Dent drive his mount. Yes, they would help. They would leave even now. In the teeth of the storm they saddled hurriedly. Then a fearful bolt struck close. The herders fell stunned and the Englishman, dead.

Two mornings later, the searchers reached Dent's camp. Under a brush arbor lay the body of his wife, dead in childbirth . . . but obviously delivered.

In horror they saw more. All about were tracks of the lobo. The body of Mollie was marked with cuts. But the child was gone.

A decade passed, and the now-American military road swung north up the canyon past the site of Dent's old camp; and along that trail came the Forty-Niners' wagons, like those Camp Hudson's sergeant would remember. After them marched solitary little wilderness cabins and, finally, remote ranches. And as each of them came, the tale of the lost Dent child was passed along.

The story had grown to fearful proportions. Something ran the night out there, a creature resembling a half-grown girl, yet something that crouched and snarled within its wolf pack. Seminole scouts, up from Fort Clark—long after Camp Hudson was abandoned—had read wolf sign and, along with it, the unmistakable print of human hand and foot.

Finally, the old story claims, this remote frontier gathered its forces to track down the pack. Out from the canyon they threw a cordon against a wilderness that is still there today; they closed, and finally cut out their quarry.

There was a near-human form and face, something capable of rising almost erect, yet more agile on all fours—a growling, cowering creature that could utter no sound beyond the chilling cry of the wolf. Within a shed, they locked the thing.

Inside the house, the few women shut themselves in a bedroom; let their men face the terrible sound rising from the night all about. The wolves were coming! They were in the corral! Out rushed the men to save their stock. Out, yelling hoarsely, firing at a blur of darting forms that vanished into dark silence. Part of the shed had been ripped away. The wolf girl was gone.

Over the years, reports of the wolf woman lessened. Some thought the pack had withdrawn into rougher backcountry due to the gold miners. Others, when pressed, believed they had glimpsed something near the water—something that ran like a wolf but watched you with a human face. And not one, but two . . . maybe more.

That was almost a century ago, along that lonely reach of river, and I have been unable to find anyone who admits to the existence of such a creature. That kind of thinking belongs with old fables, such as those that tell of witches and ghosts and evil spirits inhabiting human forms, not to mention strange beings from space.

For my part, I have dismissed the whole matter as little more than a highly imaginative legend, and I hope you will do the same thing.

However, next time you travel that canyon by night, stop at one of the river crossings, preferably the one where a granite marker tells of forgotten Camp Hudson. Wait in the dark and listen.

Perhaps, as it happened the last time I camped up there, you'll hear it . . . the long, cold cry of the coyote. Or could it be that of the gray wolf, supposedly extinct?

Could it be . . . ? Of course, it was probably my imagination, but does it sound almost human to you?

EDITOR'S NOTE: John Dent was a trapper, but he was also on the run for murder. He was wanted in Georgia for the killing of a fellow trapper.

He had come to Texas to hide, and took his very pregnant wife into the wilderness to stay hidden and make money.

The sightings of the wolf girl began in 1845. In 1852, there was a sighting of the girl breastfeeding two wolf pups. If it were the Dent daughter, she would have been seventeen at this time. This was the last reported physical sighting of her.

However, sightings of a more disturbing kind were reported up to the 1930s. These were of wolves with odd, human-like faces. And while physically improbable, it is interesting.

LADY IN DISTRESS

Neches River

The woman relaxed in her bath—spring afternoons heated up these East Texas woodlands. She sank lower into the cool water, attempting to soothe nerves still frayed from the night before. Maybe it was her imagination, as her husband insisted. Who would trouble their pretty little home, now so quiet that she could hear distant country sounds?

Then she felt a presence in the room with her. Without moving, she raised her eyes above the rim of the tub.

Barring the bathroom door, a large man in out-of-date clothes loomed, grinning. He could almost touch her. Yet she could see the doorframe through his body.

Of course, she screamed.

This time had been different. Before, he had been invisible and whispered to her in Spanish. But he was the one, and he did not remotely belong in this place, this century. He was from a time she could not conceive of. And he had to be the one who had bothered her since she and her husband had moved here in late 1979.

Finally she had seen him—a warrior's clothing, a kind of sun-bleached uniform, a dark hat, piercing black eyes. And a sword in a brass-tipped scabbard.

"Go away!" she shouted to the emptiness.

Then she calmed. The presence was gone. Her glance swept the empty house. She must get ahold of herself. She must dress and get out. She must get help. From whom, though? Tell about this, and people would surely call her crazy.

It is for that reason, you will understand, that this story will not name her or her husband. We will call her Betty. Betty Porter and her husband, Cliff.

Her story, little known beyond immediate family.

The visitant in the Porter's home ignores men. Women, though, are another story. This ghost seems to have arisen from a past measured in centuries.

At first glance, it has chosen an unlikely dwelling, one pleasantly tucked away in the northeast forests near the Neches River. That this is old and storied land was unknown to the Porters at first, but now they have learned. Their children are grown and live elsewhere. Periodically the husband's work takes him away—something they both fear. At those times, Betty must live alone.

For their part, the Porter men—husband and sons-in-law—attempt to combat the spirit, but how do you combat something you cannot take hold of or even see? In seeking an answer to that, almost by accident, they brought me into the story.

On a November day in 1979, the Porters had found the house they wanted. With some work they could move it to the land they had bought, living in a trailer while Cliff remodeled inside and out. They placed the house beside a green spring, slowing now but attractive to them and interesting: they had been told that Natives once camped here.

Almost from the first night in the trailer, a strangeness seemed to settle from the dark—inexplicable noises from the house that waited for them. For a time, they ignored the sounds. Cliff contended that his wife was imagining them. Clearly she had heard the nicker of horses making for water. Nothing but wintery darkness awaited the beam of his flashlight.

In March of 1980, the house was ready enough, but Betty was increasingly certain that something had followed, to haunt it. While she watched, doorknobs turned, doors opened, the chandelier swung methodically, stopped abruptly. She was seeing things, Cliff argued. One night he crawled beneath the house "to fix something." But she had heard the voice below them, just as she knew he had. He was trying to ignore it.

By degrees, she could sense that she was being watched. There was no question as to what happened that early spring night. In the back bedroom, dim with its night-light, she waked with the awful certainty that someone—a man—was in the room.

The voice again, not outside, close by. For one heartbeat, rigid in the bed, she heard deep laughter. She snapped on the lamp. The room was empty.

"What is it?" Cliff stirred sleepily.

"Nothing," she said, but for a time left the light on. She knew now that the thing could come in through locked doors. More, she knew that it was coming for her.

The remodeling finished, Cliff returned to work in town. Alone, Betty did her best to resist fear. After all, daylight should repel ghosts, and her husband was home before dark. Then one day as she started for the kitchen, the voice came clear and close beside her. Unintelligible to her, the words were in Spanish. One, she recognized—*diablo*. It was time to talk to her family.

"If it's a ghost," her sister suggested, "it's supposed to answer a direct question."

Next day, Betty put the question to the ghost. "Who are you? What do you want?" Rapid Spanish responded. Then she heard herself asking, "Where did you die?" She could make out the answer. *"En los olmos."*

She found a Spanish dictionary at the library. *Olmos*. Death had come in the elms. There were elms all around the house—all along the Neches bottomland.

A nearby college could translate if she could bring them something to work with. Her tape recorder—three cassettes in all—echoed a voice, thin as though far away, words too faint to distinguish. She called the librarian again. That lady knew no way to amplify them—not enough to help. Still, she had a suggestion.

That is why my phone rang in the summer of 1980. To undertake a book on Texas ghosts, surely I must be a student of parapsychology.

The Porters' son-in-law, a well-established A&M forestry graduate, made the call. "Three months ago," he said, "I'd have laughed ghosts out of the house." Then he told me about the Porter home. He felt forced to call after what had happened to Betty in the bathroom.

It was November of 1980 before I reached Betty Porter. Nothing had changed unless perhaps to intensify. No longer did anyone—certainly not she—speak to this being; that had only increased its visitations.

When they slept, it waked them, banging furniture, setting off the smoke alarm, pulling away bedclothes. It was that man, for he let himself be seen again, once a close-passing reflection in the glass-front china cabinet Betty was polishing, once moving through the closed bathroom door. From bathroom through the kitchen to invisibility, Cliff had pursued what he called a shadow. How could you shoot a shadow?

I had promised that names would be withheld, and I had watched Betty's hands tremble, holding the notes she had made; to be sure she placed events in coherent order. Well, if I believed her, then what could I do to help?

Shortly, Cliff's work would take him away. It was that time she feared.

I could try to find them help, I told her, explaining that I was no parapsychologist.

I was historian enough to be intrigued by the spring, just outside the bathroom window, but I went into little detail. Long ago, the Spaniards had hunted Frenchmen hereabouts. This had been Cherokee homeland, and some of them could speak Spanish. It was the ground, I suspected, not the house that was disturbed.

The weeks turned and the local leads we had discussed turned up no psychic help. Cliff was still there, and the youngest daughter had moved in for a time, but, a young wife, she must leave for her own home. This pretty girl immediately had shared the visitant's attentions, nightly, close beside her bed. Raising her voice drove him away.

At this juncture, I called a psychic friend far removed from those woodlands. (Helen's story is told elsewhere in this book in "The Foreteller"). She wanted only briefest details, none of my conclusions: parapsychology demands to see for itself. Yes, she would help, get someone to go there if it became necessary.

When I talked again with Helen, she said, "I don't see a Spaniard; I see an Indian." For a moment she paused. "It isn't going to be easy. I think you'd better have her call me."

At the time of original publication, this home remained troubled, in need of some sort of divine intervention, according to Helen. Since publicity is as disturbing to the Porters as is their visitant, quiet help—to bless the home and exorcise the being—is needed. I will refer valid volunteers (no fee can be involved). The lady is still in distress, and probably cannot do it alone.

And so, in a sense, I am out of it, except for historical surmise. Could it be a Spanish dragoon from that terrible winter of 1691, one who froze, hunting the French? Could it be the Native that Helen sees?

The Porters' spring is close indeed to the Cherokees' last night camp before being driven from Texas in a running battle up the nearby Neches River. That year was 1839.

It was in this camp that Chief Bowles, commanding the Cherokee, sent word to a Texas army just south: he would not retreat; he would stand and fight. It was here that he strapped on the sword that Sam Houston had given him, and then went out to die in the elms along Neches.

But that is simply history, and this, yet an unfinished story.

INDEX OF NAMES AND PLACES